WHAT TO SAY WHEN WE PRAY: *Finding Power in the Lord's Prayer.*

by

Dr. Robert E. Palmer

Desert Ministries Press
Matthews, North Carolina

WHAT TO SAY WHEN WE PRAY: FINDING POWER IN THE LORD'S PRAYER

First Edition 2010

© Copyright 2010 by
Desert Ministries Inc.
P.O. Box 747
Matthews, North Carolina 28106
ISBN 0-914733-38-9
ISBN UPC # 978-0-914733-38-6

Printed by Eagle Graphic Services
Fort Lauderdale, Florida

DEDICATED

To Mary Lou,
My constant companion
and supporter.

TABLE OF CONTENTS

PUBLISHER'S INTRODUCTION

I am pleased to write this little introduction to Dr. Palmer's book on Prayer. No matter when and where Christian people gather to talk over their spiritual concerns, the topic of utmost interest is almost always on prayer and how to make prayer more effective. The Bible tells us that we can have direct access to the One Eternal God through Jesus Christ who came to earth to be One with us. The question then becomes how can we most fully tap into that power and make our lives more effective in his service.

Bob Palmer has been preaching and practicing Prayer for a long time. Early in his ministry, also long ago, he published a little book on The Lord's Prayer which became widely popular in the later middle years of the Twentieth Century. Since I have been traveling that road step by step, I have been helped by his faithful and may I say "folksy" approach to the pulpit and in this case on what we should say when we pray. In publishing this current volume, I was pleased to see that his sense of humor has not diminished one iota. As he writes in the book, the response of laughter in the pews means at least that God's people are listening, and he likens it to the sound of a great Amen.

You will notice that some of the time Dr. Palmer has retained the jargon of those former years. As a lover of fine literature he refuses to abandon the majesty of the King James Translation. At times I had to stop and think about what he was saying and how the changing ideas of the modern church members might view it. But it was like music to my ears to hear of "Thine" and "Thou" and "Thee et al." But, you will also notice that he has balanced his traditional attitudes with a healthy respect for the viable changes through the days and decades of his ministry. He retains his healthy call for a renewal and deepening of our commitment to Jesus Christ.

My hope is that you will be touched by the message of these chapters and be brought down to earth by what he says. In our Desert Ministries' materials we seek to bring The Living Water of Jesus Christ into the lives of those who are forced to live in the deserts of human life. At the end of this book we have listed some of the materials we provide to churches and pastors and laity without charge.

What better way to find that "Living Water" than in a fruitful prayer life which taps us into the source of the power we need to survive in the living of these days? One of the benefits of this book is to look over the ways in which a prominent pastor has changed and grown in the way he searches for the hidden meanings of The Lord's Prayer. I commend Dr. Palmer's book to you in hope that you will enjoy its merrie journey through a familiar Prayer, and that when you are through, you will be empowered to understand more about The Lord's Prayer and then to reach out into the lives of those who have lost touch with their prayerful roots – and to enjoy it all as you go on.

Meanwhile, God bless you and keep you in His care.

Cordially,

Rev. Richard M. Cromie, President
Desert Ministries, Inc.
Charlotte, North Carolina

AUTHOR'S PREFACE

I was surprised when I saw in the Smithsonian magazine an advertisement for a "Stunning Cross... hold it to the light and the Lord's Prayer is revealed!" I write this volume on What to Say When We Pray, in the hope and with the prayer that you may find deeper meanings revealed when you study each word in the Lord's Prayer. That is, by holding up the Lord's Prayer to the light that is Jesus Christ, his words and deeds are revealed.

While many volumes have been written about this subject, I believe some new light may be shed as I share my reflections after a lifetime of praying this prayer daily. Earlier in my ministry I penned a brief book called Our Prayer. The present book is offered at the end of almost sixty years of ministry as an update and summary of my thoughts.

When I retired from my last large church, I found that I lacked the space at home to retain my extensive library and filed resources and was forced to give them away. Thus, I am here unable to list foot notes or give sufficient credit for some sources I have quoted. For this I apologize to any author not properly credited.

For some time I, and the congregations I have served, have benefited from the Desert Ministries, Inc. resources. This book is a direct result of an invitation from the founder of Desert Ministries, a good friend and a great preacher, Richard M. Cromie. To him I am extremely indebted for his assistance in helping share my thoughts.

Bob Palmer
Celebration, Florida
Autumn 2009

1

Lord, Teach us to Pray

"Lord, teach us to pray" was the explicit request of the disciples and the implicit longing of Christians today. Undoubtedly, you have prayed the same prayer at some time in your life. Yet, though you pray it sincerely, too often it seems that your prayer is not answered. Jesus promised that if we ask for "anything in his name," he will give it to us. And yet it does not happen. At times we know our prayers are selfish or even childish, but at other times the prayer is spoken honestly and sincerely, and we wonder why it is not answered.

In this, you are not so very different from anyone else, even the disciples of Jesus Christ. They too, did not know what they really believed about prayer. Much that they had heard called prayer did not fit in with their notions of God, and life and the universe, far less in what Jesus was teaching them day by day. Still, observing what Jesus said and did, they felt there must be such a thing as purposeful prayer, and if there is a God Who is concerned for His creation and His children, then surely there must be some way to develop a two-way communication with Him.

Most Christians face these same kinds of questions about prayer. Some have been disappointed with life and have given up any hope that divine help is available. One problem is that when we pray to God today I suspect we are troubled by certain features of our modern world which did not trouble Jesus' disciples when they first heard this prayer. For one thing, our concept of the universe in which God seems remote in its vastness was unknown to them. Their cosmogony imagined earth as limited space, with heaven up above and hell somewhere beneath. We have science with its natural laws which seem to rule out any "miracles." Further, we have modern psychology which speaks of religion in terms of escape or projection. And there is our society with all its modern enticements to attract our attention and distract our best intentions.

All of us suffer from the fact that the Lord's Prayer has become so familiar to us that we repeat it without a genuine understanding of what its words truly mean. As Shakespeare put it: "Our words fly up to heaven; our thoughts remain below." From the cradle to the grave we have repeated the Prayer. All the more reason therefore, why we need some fresh insight as to the need and nature of private and public communication with God.

What we need to do, therefore, is what the disciples did—seek the guidance of Jesus Christ for our understanding of prayer. The gospels clearly show how prayer was a source of power in his life, an experience as natural as breathing, as much to be expected as sleep and food. That is why they asked him: "Lord, teach us to pray." The significance of this request is heightened since this is the only recorded request by the disciples for Jesus to teach them anything.

Jesus' answer to his disciples, and to us, is the Lord's Prayer. In response, he said, "This is how you should pray." He did not say, "This is why you should pray." Most people try to pray at some point in their lives, but they do not know what to say. What can be said? Jesus does not offer any particular techniques of prayer. Apart from his comment about going into a room alone and closing the door, he doesn't concern himself with the precise manner in which we pray. The "how" refers to what we should say when we want to talk with God. This is what Jesus gives us, and it strikes me there is value for us in trying to understand better the implications of each word he gives us in this model prayer.

The Lord's Prayer is probably the most familiar passage in the Bible. For nearly 2,000 years, millions of people have been reciting it billions of times. It is only sixty-six words in the King James Version and can be recited in less than a minute. Like many of you, I repeated it as a child and I suspect that it may be the last words I utter before I die. I have a habit of saying it daily, sometimes reverently and with deep meaning, at other times it comes routinely and carelessly, without thinking of its meanings. Yet, there is power throughout these words and a beauty and a serenity which take us above and beyond words. It can reassure our hearts, strengthen our resolve and lead us into a more personal contact with God our Father.

There is much that the disciples might have learned about prayer from Jesus' own practice of prayer. Sometimes he prayed alone, at other times he invited them to pray with him. They were certainly a diverse group in profession, personality, temperament and background. In fact, about the only thing that seemed to tie them together was their attraction to the person of Jesus. They discerned a charisma or dynamic or godliness about him in what he said and did. But there was one segment of his conduct that especially commanded their attention – his prayer life. No wonder they came and asked him to teach them to pray.

Jesus' answer was not a pat formula. He was showing his disciples the best approach to prayer—a pattern if you will. He was giving them their priorities in prayer, which in turn would become their priorities in life.

During the fifty-eight years of my active ministry I have sensed that I must answer at least two questions worshippers are pondering as they enter church: "Is there a God? Does He care for me?" The Lord's Prayer can answer both of these questions in the affirmative. The Lord's Prayer does not answer all our questions about the origins of prayer or the study of comparative religion. It reveals a secret of Jesus' power – he invites us into a new religious experience of God.

When we search for the uniqueness and singular power of Jesus' life we will find it where his disciples did. It was not just in his words or actions, not in his parables or miracles, not even in his crucifixion. His disciples sensed it was in his life of prayer, his new religious experience and so they asked him, "Lord, teach us to pray."

While we read in the gospels of Jesus' frequent prayers, we have almost no account of what he actually said when he prayed. On the Mount of Transfiguration, he spoke not only to his heavenly Father, but also to Moses and Elijah. In the Garden of Gethsemane he prayed, "Oh my Father, if it be possible, let this cup pass from me." Time and again, he went to be alone in prayer, and even when he prayed in the presence of his disciples, we know only a few of his words. Often we hear his words, "Thy will." And once as he prayed his face was so transfigured that even his garments were luminous. One thing is certain; his prayers were a vital part of his life. No wonder the disciples asked, "Lord, teach us to pray."

There are evidences of Jesus teaching about prayer by example throughout the four gospels. The fact that he repeatedly referred to prayer and practiced prayers is even more significant when we realize that not more than one hundred, and perhaps as few as forty of the days he lived as an adult on earth receive any mention by the Gospel writers.

What he says about prayer is to strengthen our own prayer life, and encourage us to be expectant. "Ask and it shall be given you; seek and you shall find; knock and it shall be opened unto you." "If you have faith as a grain of mustard seed, you shall say to this mountain, remove hence to yonder place and it shall remove, and nothing shall be impossible unto you. What things so ever you desire, when you pray, believe that you receive them and you shall have them."

Jesus also taught that prayer must be humble, not boastful as if we were able to accomplish something by ourselves. We are to pray in a spirit of humility, acknowledging that prayer is a gift of God. We are to pray "In Jesus name." That is, after the nature of Jesus, using his example when we pray. There is no place for self-righteousness in our prayers, as Jesus taught in his parable of the Pharisee and the publican.

Jesus taught that prayer must be real. It must not be ostentatious, like sounding a trumpet in the streets. Prayer must be more than a repetition of words, more than vain repetitions or empty pretenses. Prayers are to be offered in secret, in a private place. Yet, prayer should be offered as well when we are going about our daily activities, hallowing the common things.

Jesus also taught his followers to be persistent in our prayers, not giving up after the first effort, as in the case of the poor murderer pleading before the heartless judge, or in the parable of the man knocking on his neighbor's door at midnight asking a favor.

It seems all the other things Jesus taught about prayer are focused in the specific answer of the Lord's Prayer he uttered when the disciples implored him, "Lord, teach us to pray." Thus, it is well worth our while to look afresh at each phrase of the Lord's Prayer in discovering what new meanings await us.

However, to call this the Lord's Prayer is technically a misnomer, since the prayer is clearly designed for the use of his followers. For surely, he did not need to request forgiveness for sin. For this reason I have called this book, What To Say When We Pray. I often discover when I try to pray that I am at a loss for words. Then I ask myself if I am being selfish. Are my requests too limited in scope? Do I have the right to ask for certain things?

To these concerns our Lord responds by reminding us to pray to God as our dear Father. In so doing, Jesus summarizes all we need to know about Christian theology. The prayer speaks of the holiness of our Father, the coming of His kingdom, the provision for those who seek His kingdom, amnesty for everyone's wrong doing and deliverance from all evil.

It staggers the mind to realize this prayer is being constantly uttered every moment by millions of people in thousands of languages every day. All the more reason that we must be sure that our prayers are meant to accomplish their intended purpose for the glory of God.

Beginning with the outline of the prayer and continuing with the chapters which explain each of the phrases in the prayer, this book is written in the hope that you may make it your prayer, not only by repeating it often, but by ordering your thoughts, attitudes and actions in terms of the framework it offers for Christian living.

Our Father Who art in heaven, from Whom cometh every good prayer, and Who hath given us a model prayer whereby we may be guided aright in our communion and companionship with Thee, while our eyes have not beheld Thee, we have known One so holy and lovely that He could convincingly say: "He that hath seen me hath seen the Father."

O God, Thou dost seem so intimate in Thy nearness and yet so infinite in Thy greatness, that when we look up to Thee Who is perfect, we feel impelled to add, *Hallowed be Thy Name*. It follows naturally. With reverence we recognize God's Name to be glorious over all the earth.

We know, too, that You who causes the stars to swing so perfectly in the heavens desires also to sway the people of the earth, for Jesus taught us to pray: *Thy Kingdom come, Thy will be done on earth as it is in heaven*. Our stubborn wills have been unwilling to receive Thy Kingdom. Yet our hope of its coming does not die. Help us, O God, to be worthy citizens of Thy Kingdom. Give us the grace to surrender our wills to Your will. Make our vision clear to see Your holy Will and Purpose.

If we are to serve as Your children in bringing Your kingdom on earth, we must have strength, and so we pray, *give us this day our daily bread*. We believe all of our needs are of concern to Thee for Thou hast made us with these hungers and thirsts. We are not expecting You to answer all our desires: we ask only that You will give us what we need; believing that if we seek Your good and the good of all, there will be more than enough for all.

Even as we pray for our daily bread, we are mindful that because we have not put Thy Kingdom first, many of Your children are in misery and want and sin. Please then *forgive us our debts as we forgive our debtors.* We try to forget our sins but we cannot forgive ourselves, because we are not our own. But we try to belong to Your whole Family but our sins separate us from You and Your other children. So grant us the spirit of forgiveness, even as we have been forgiven by You in Your mercy.

In so praying, we think of tomorrow and also ask, *Lead us not into temptation.* We would not presume on Thy fatherly goodness by repeatedly falling into sin. Help us to say "no" to the suggestion of sin because the substance of it appears. But, since we still must face sin, we pray, *deliver us from evil.*

For *Thine is the Kingdom.* Though wayward and wicked people may try to live without Thee, Thy rule of righteousness is here waiting. And *Thine is the power.* Though the love which lay in the manger and hung on the Cross looks fragile, it is the force which always sustains and ultimately prevails. And *Thine is the glory.* Though the paths of man's glory lead but to the grave, Thine is everlasting and the path for those forgiven in Jesus Christ is forever and ever. We pray this and every prayer, "Through Jesus Christ our Lord and Redeemer." As a sign of our affirmation of all this, we say *Amen.*

&&&&&&&

I conclude this introduction with a prayer based upon the Lord's Prayer which I discovered some years ago and have often found helpful. I hope it will be helpful to you.

I cannot say OUR
    if my religion has no room for other people and their needs.

I cannot say FATHER
  if I do not demonstrate this relationship in my daily living.
I cannot say WHO ART IN HEAVEN
  if all my interests and pursuits are in earthly things.
I cannot say HALLOWED BE THY NAME
  if I, who am called by His name, am not holy.
I cannot say THY WILL BE DONE
  if I am unwilling or resentful of having it in my own life.
I cannot say ON EARTH AS IT IS IN HEAVEN
  unless I am truly ready to give myself to His service here
  and now.
I cannot say GIVE US THIS DAY OUR DAILY BREAD
  if I ignore the genuine needs of my neighbors.
I cannot say FORGIVE US OUR DEBTS AS WE FORGIVE
  OUR DEBTORS
  if I continue to harbor a grudge against anyone.
I cannot say LEAD US NOT INTO TEMPTATION
  if I deliberately choose to remain in a situation where I am
  likely to be tempted.
I cannot say DELIVER US FROM EVIL
  if I am not prepared to stand for the right.
I cannot say THINE IS THE KINGDOM
  if I fear what my neighbors and friends may say or do.
I cannot say THINE IS THE POWER
  if I do not open my heart to receive the power of God in Jesus
  Christ and show that power through loving others.
I cannot say THINE IS THE GLORY
  if I am seeking my own glory first.
I cannot say FOREVER
  if I am anxious about each day's affairs.
I cannot say AMEN
  unless I can honestly say, "Whatever it will cost, this is
  my prayer."

2

How to Get Close to God

Someone challenged a friend, "I'll bet ten dollars you can't say the Lord's Prayer from beginning to end." His friend answered, "I'll take that bet." He began: "Now I lay me down to sleep, I pray the Lord my soul to keep. If I should die before I wake, I pray the Lord my soul to take." When he had finished, there was a pause and his friend grinned. "Well, I'll be, you did know it!" and he handed him the ten dollars.

We would not have made such a mistake, of course, for we have been repeating the Lord's Prayer for years. Yet its very familiarity can dull our spirits to the fullness of its rich meaning. It comes trippingly on the tongue, and in the routine, its clauses fall from our lips without catching hold of our hearts. It is often committed to memory, but it is not always learned by heart. It is frequently repeated, but rarely obeyed.

Therefore, let us attempt to reduce this oft repeated prayer to the tempo of a slow motion picture that we may follow the movement of its thought, catch the shades of its meaning and thus enter into a closer communion with our heavenly Father.

I once attended a conference where each of us was given the opportunity to utilize some spiritual mantra, or saying, that we would repeat over and over silently to ourselves. The mantra that I took was this: "Our Father." It was amazing how the more I said it the more I became aware of the significance of those simple words. I came to realize that it is not really the Lord's Prayer. When Jesus taught it to his disciples and in turn to us: it became "Our" prayer. It is the kind of prayer he expects us to say.

The account of this prayer in the gospel according to Matthew suggests that Jesus gave this prayer as a model— "after this manner..." Luke presents it with a slightly different emphasis: he suggests that Jesus intended it as a form – "when ye pray..." Perhaps it serves as both a model and a form. At any rate, it is not so much an excursion into theology, as it is an adoration from the soul. Luke tells us that the disciples saw Jesus praying and asked Him then and there to teach them how to pray. They knew that Jesus embodied the very power of God, and they knew that this power in Jesus was partly traceable to His prayers. So they made the request, "Lord, teach us to pray."

Jesus' answer to His disciples begins with the words, "OUR Father." We must not slide over the pronoun. This very first word fractures the hermit's life. It means that as God has reconciled the world to Himself through Christ, you and I need to be reconciled to Him through faith, reconciled to one another through love and reconciled to ourselves through acceptance. This plural prayer is not for an only child, but for a brotherhood—the human family. It smashes the barriers of discrimination, breaks down the walls of exclusiveness; it bursts the little whispering circles and shouts a hearty welcome to all.

Oliver Wendell Holmes once said that these two opening words were the sum and substance of his religion: "Our Father."

The Christian religion may be likened to a triangle with God at the apex, yourself at one of the angles and your neighbor at the other. The closer that you come to God, the closer you will be to your neighbor, and the greater the distance from your neighbor, the further you will be from God. Basic to any relationship to our neighbor, however, is our prior relationship to our Lord. "We loved because he first loved us."

A man who had spent some considerable time in prison came to his minister and said, "I do not want much in life. I only want to belong again." This is what we all want—to belong. And so to pray, "Our Father," means that we will strive to remove all barriers and recognize everyone else as a child of God. Despite the book title, Live Alone and Like IT, such a venture would be doomed. And I understand that even the author of this book later married and rejoined society.

Broadly speaking, God's children are divided into two groups: Those who recognize the Fatherhood of God and enter into the enjoyment of it, and those who do not. Jesus said to certain proud Pharisees, "You are of your father the devil." They were sons of God by creation, but they were not claiming their birthright. The Apostle John declares, "As many as received Him, to them gave He power to become the children of God." Therefore, we hear His joyful shout across the years: "Behold, what manner of love the Father hath bestowed upon us, that we should be called the children of God."

Surely this is a lesson that the Church of today needs to take to heart. As narrow as it may seem, the finest service that you and I can render to our world is to love each other. If our Lord cannot make a brotherhood out of the Church, how can we ever pray with integrity for Him to make a brotherhood out of the wide world? If we ourselves do not love our neighbors whom we have seen, how can we love those whom we have not seen?

The whole Church, then, is included in this little word "our." For a man to assert that he can be a Christian without the Church is as foolish as for him to imagine that an arm can live without its body. The Lord's Prayer in its very first word reminds us that God is concerned not only with the continuing spirit and influence of the community of believers known as the Church. It is true that corporate prayer would grow thin if each man did not pray in secret; but it is also true that personal prayer would die of loneliness and perhaps of lovelessness, if it knew no social bonds.

Further, no one has the right to take Jesus' words, "Our Father" upon his lips unless he is prepared to treat not only fellow Christians, but all men and women everywhere as members of one and the same family.

When Jesus implanted this conviction of brotherhood in people's hearts, it was not merely a law of brotherliness He was giving, but also an adequate motive for all men and women to belong together. To be able to say to one another - "that one like me has God for Father; he/she too is a child of God" - is to be well on the way to vanquishing all feelings of superiority.

When we go into the theater with our ticket of admission, the usher tears it in half and hands us the stub. On the stub is written the letters "Void if detached." That can be written across the life of any Christian. We are really not good for much if we are detached from the Body of Christ which is God's family. We are here on earth because we have family ties to be nurtured and shared. When Jesus implanted this conviction of God as our Father and all of us as members of His family, it was not because he was giving merely a law of how we are to live. He was giving a motive for living; he was seeking to influence our hearts as well as our actions.

Here, at least, the dictum that "East is East and West is West and ne'er the twain shall meet" breaks down; here divergences of temperament are transcended, and jarring prejudices give way; here denominationalism falls into its true perspective, and all discords that spoil the spiritual music are harmonized; here the deep cleavages of race and nationality are removed. Something far more grand and noble begins to come into view—the family of God. Here, in Jesus' revelation of God as our Father, the hope of a unified earth has been given once and for all.

The second word tells us that God is our FATHER. Others previously to the gospels had hinted at this; but only Jesus Christ dared to go so far to claim Him as such for every man, and only Jesus Christ was able to live out consistently and triumphantly the kind of life that a vital sense of the divine Fatherhood should imply. What good is an impersonal God? This prayer is a child's confession, and the rest of the prayer is pointless until we make the prodigal's decision his own: "I will arise and go to my father."

Perhaps the most amazing truth in the development of my own Christian faith stems from our Lord's calling God "Father". He even goes so far in doing this that he uses the word "Abba" or "daddy" in referring to God. Just imagine the God of the universe, the Creator of all things eternal and almighty, being referred to as "Daddy."

This becomes even more significant when I read about Jesus' other comments about parent-child relationships. He speaks of fathers as "being evil" (Matthew7:9-11). He knows how fathers can be limited by their earthly circumstances. He even goes so far as to say, "Call no man your father on earth for you have one father" who is in heaven (Matt 23:9).

A father's blessing was very important in the Bible, as seen in the story of Jacob and Esau. However, not even the blessing of an exemplary father was sufficient. Jesus knew that only our heavenly Father is sufficient for our basic needs, and so he teaches us to call God, "Father".

Within the short compass of our Gospels, Jesus refers to God as "Father" more than one hundred and fifty times. It is there in the first recorded boyhood utterances of Jesus, "Do you not know that I must be about my Father's business?" It is still there in his final cry on the cross: "Father, into Thy hands I commend my spirit."

We hear a good deal today from psychologists about a "father image". Because of Jesus we shall forever conceive of the Lord of the Universe in the image of "Our Father."

The main thing in prayer is not that we present particular petitions but that we enter into communion, into a personal relationship with the Father. If I do nothing else but say from the bottom of my heart, "Our Father," the most important thing has already happened.

Of all the names or titles possible, Jesus addressed God as Father, Abba. Jesus certainly was not suggesting sentimental childishness in our relationship with God. The term Abba emerges from a family context, and suggests a mix of affection, respect, mutual responsibilities and love. The radical character of Jesus' giving of "Abba" as an address to God lies in its astonishing claim about the relationship of the Holy One of Israel to the disciples.

The Lord's Prayer unflinchingly insists that the same God who is creator, infinitely greater than we are, capable of delivering us or not, forgiving us or not, and of bringing the world to its consummation, can also be addressed by us with the easy intimacy of a child with its parents. Obedience and confidence, affection and discipline, certain faith and eager service describe the relationship with God as Abba.

I'm aware that we are living in the 21st Century with its emphasis on gender and other discrimination. I have friends who insist on referring to "Our Mother," who art in Heaven. For me, while there is femininity and masculinity in God, yet it is Jesus Christ, God's Son, who, giving us a model, says, "Pray as if you were praying to a loving, kind, benevolent, wise, caring and powerful Father." Only Jesus Christ dared to say this. The main thing in prayer for us as Christians is not that we present particular petitions and requests, but that we enter into a relationship as members of God's family. If it helps your faith to refer to God in the feminine pronoun, so be it. It is the parental relationship which is paramount.

John Ruskin, the art critic, was right when he said that the world was an orphanage so long as men do not know God as their Father, and all wisdom and knowledge are mere bewildered darkness if they do not teach us to love Him.

By calling God "Father" we declare that our faith rests securely, not just upon a belief in God, but upon the comforting assurance that God loves His children to the point of redemption and watches over them as a father watches over his children. To call God "Father" is at the foundation of all of our beliefs. The word "Father" is the gateway to the consciousness of God. It is the starting point of Christian prayer.

An American missionary was teaching an Indian woman the Lord's Prayer. When he had finished his explanation of the first phrase, "Our Father." she said, "I don't need to know any more. If God is our Father that is enough."

While the prayer speaks of God as Father, it must be remembered that it was in a time and a place where paternal authority stood much higher than it does in modern times. Love between father and son, or mother and daughter, means essentially authoritative love on the one side and obedient love on the other. The father uses his authority to shape the child into the sort of human being he wants the son to be. God the Father is doubtless more intellectually our superior than a proud father is of his small son whom he watches crawling on a bear rug. But on Christ's authority we can say that the relationship is the same.

Third, Jesus said that God is not only our Father; He is our Father IN HEAVEN.

This reference to heaven has made many moderns apprehensive as they strive to be "honest to God." It is true that men in Jesus' day operated with a picture of the universe startlingly different from ours, but it has been too readily assumed that they all had a simple literal picture of heaven, earth and hell – the "three story universe" some theologians talk about. If Jesus had said instead, "Our Father who art the ground of all being," this would somehow have made it respectable to them.

By saying God is in heaven, Jesus does not mean to locate God. Those who think of God as being in heaven only, can end up thinking of God as being distant and far away. This conception has crept into many of our songs. "There is a happy land, far, far away." How did we get this conception?

Certainly not from the New Testament! When Jesus was talking to Nicodemus, he said, "No man hath ascended up to heaven, but He that came down from heaven, even the Son of man who is in heaven." That is, Jesus claimed that while he was sitting and talking to this rabbi, he himself was actually in heaven.

This means that heaven is here and now, as well as away and in the future. This means that God's kingdom goes beyond the earth. This means that we are not what we ought to be. And so we point our spires toward the sky.

When Jesus says, "Who art in heaven," He is describing God. Heaven is synonymous with perfection. Jesus might have said, "Our perfect Father," and it would have meant the same thing. Heaven is the place of perfection. Jesus is telling us, therefore, that God is not only our Father, He is the perfect Father.

The appeal of the word "Father" depends upon the pictures that it brings to your mind. Though it may not be a beautiful word to everyone, to most of us it means fond memories. For me, the word "Father" connotes love and understanding, care and concern. The word "Father" flashes before my mind a thousand and one pictures I like to remember.

Now, Jesus said, "Take fatherhood at its best and lift it into the realm of the infinite, and you will have some conception of God." He is our heavenly Father. He is perfect in His knowledge of us. He knows what we need before we ask Him. Because He knows, He sometimes has to refuse our foolish and selfish requests. He is perfect in His love, eager to answer our prayers.

God is also perfect in His ability. Sometimes, we face situations where we would give our very lives to help someone, but we cannot. But if we give Him the opportunity, He can and will help us. We sometimes cry with that desperate father who brought his son to Jesus, "Lord, if Thou canst do anything, have mercy upon us and help us." Jesus said, "You have put the "if" in the wrong place. If you can believe, all things are possible to him that believeth." He is our perfect Father.

"Our Father, who art in heaven." If we had only these six words, we would have a suitable "Lord's Prayer." The other sixty two words Jesus gave in the prayer are by way of explanation.

These six words remind us of Jesus' story of a young man in The Parable of the Prodigal Son, who thought he might find life better away from his father. And so he said to his father, "Give me what I have coming," and he left for a distant land. While there, however, he realized the mistake he had made. He remembered that he was still his father's son, and that his father loved him, and longed for him to come back and claim his birthright. So one day the young man said, "I will return to my father." And when his father saw him, he welcomed him home. Jesus not only taught this lesson, he demonstrated it with his life and death, and thereby enables each of us now to come in faith to our Father who is in heaven.

Many people today speak of the Fatherhood of God as though it were axiomatic. How can we do this on a planet permeated with perplexity, a society split by struggles, homes haunted with hatred, and through it all the uncertain tenure of the hold we have on life. All of these things cry out against the concept of a Loving Heavenly Father?

The only way to answer this question decisively is through an acceptance of Jesus Christ as the Savior of your soul and the Lord of your life. You will never be absolutely certain that a loving Father is on the throne of the universe until you have met the redeeming grace of Jesus Christ in the secret place of your own soul.

On a certain occasion, some friends were discussing the features of the great Scottish writer, Sir Walter Scott. One who had known him quite intimately remarked that the very best portraits did little justice to the great writer's face which always wore such a radiant expression. He commented, "In the best portraits the luster is there indeed, but somehow or other it needs lighting up."

This is a suggestive phrase. In the Old Testament portraits of God, the luster was there indeed, but similar to the portraits of Scott, it needed Jesus Christ to light it up. Jesus lit up our understanding of God when he taught us to pray, "Our Father, who art in heaven." Once you can do this, life becomes not a lonely road but a wonderful partnership, and the world becomes not a cruel battlefield but our Father's Home. You still have to walk through the darkness but there is someone there who knows the way and who will hold your hand.

"I know He is, and what He is,
Whose one great purpose is
The good of all.
I rest my soul on His
Immortal love and Fatherhood;
And trust Him, as His children should."
ANONYMOUS

Prayer: *Our Heavenly Father, as we learn to trust You and believe that you care for us all, help us to pray as members of one human family who are certain of their Father's love, as demonstrated daily by our bountiful blessings, and as shown supremely by the loving forgiveness of Jesus Christ, your son, our Lord. Amen.*

3

DOES GOD KNOW YOU BY NAME?

A little child knelt by her bed one night, misunderstanding the opening words of the Prayer, said, "Our Father, who art in heaven, how did you know my name?" For me, this is one of the two questions I ask when I enter a worship service. First I ask myself if God is real. And then I want to know if He knows me by name.

When I visit churches, I like to arrive early and take an order of service and familiarize myself with what's going to happen in advance. On one such occasion, I entered the church and noticed that the first hymn was one of my favorite Welsh tunes, "Immortal, Invisible God." But someone mistakenly printed the title as "Immoral, Invisible God." I chuckled at it and thought do we take God lightly? That's why Jesus, as soon as he taught us our prayer, "Our Father, who art in heaven," lest we become too chummy with the Almighty or take for granted that which is not ours, added "Hallowed be thy name." I.e., Thy name be holy.

This is not a remote, theological idea. It is one of the most practical concerns we have. It leads to what Albert Schweitzer called "a reverence for life." I would even submit that one of the reasons why America is having the problems it is having in terms of morality and violence is that, once having lost a sense of the holiness of God and, looking at ourselves, rather than seeing our bodies as the temples of the Holy Spirit, they became mere bundles of bones and blood, things to be satiated with drugs and chemicals and smoke and abuse. Once we lose the holiness of God, we look at love and it turns into lust, and safe sex, and condom advertisements. Once we lose the sense of the holiness of God, Sunday becomes the weekend. Hymns of praise become rock and roll. Holy writ becomes the comics and instead of sitting before an altar with bread and wine, we sit before the tube with beer and pretzels. Without the holiness of God, learning becomes education, which degenerates into seeking better grades, with the end result of guards and guns and gangs ruling our schools. I submit that when we pray, "Hallowed be thy name, it's almost like a religious reflex; we don't realize what we are saying. So please, with me look at this phrase in slow motion.

I was once travelling on a Caribbean cruise on one of those six-storied hotels they call a cruise ship, awesome, with staterooms, and hot showers, swimming pools, theaters, and dance bands, elegant restaurants, food superbly served. I went out on the fore deck one night and looked at God's heaven, with the moon and the stars, and then at the ocean with the reflections of the whites of the skylights and all the majesty of the rolling waves. It was awesome. I thought of that old British prayer: "O Lord, thy sea so great, my boat so small."

"Hallowed be thy name" – we often do not understand what we say. But because we are holy and precious and created in the image of God, he knows our name and our need, we can find those luminous moments when God and His world are holy.

Yet, for of all the phrases that trip from our tongues in

prayer could we find one more conventional: Hallowed be thy name? If a student of psychology wanted an expression which would exemplify a speech-reflex in public worship could he find one better? Here, surely, is an illustration of a mere sound-pattern to which we attach little meaning. Let us, therefore, examine what meaning we can find in the words, "Hallowed be Thy Name."

First, to HALLOW God's Name means to treat it with reverence. The phrase might be considered in relation to the second commandment, "Thou shalt not take the name of the Lord thy God in vain." What is there stated negatively, is here stated positively.

What does it mean to "take the name of the Lord in vain"? You have heard people blaspheme God, like for example even on television I heard them say, "Goddammit!" Now God may damn some things. But some people go around damning other people as though they were God. This is blasphemy. But it is not only the words that blaspheme; it is the spirit which insists that "My will be done. If I were God, I would see that this was done." This is taking the name of the Lord our God in vain.

Fortunately, God does not answer these prayers! And how thankful we should be every day we live that many of our prayers God does not answer. I do not mean the prayers we say on our knees, I mean the prayers we say so causally in our hearts and dreams. "You will call upon Me and I will not answer," says the Lord of hosts. Thank God! We wonder why a good God permits such a bad world in which His will is not done. We spend our time glorifying our own names and have not the slightest concern about glorifying His.

What an effrontery against God that we should speak this way! Yet, as Stephen Carter says in his book The Culture of Disbelief, "It's all right if we speak the name of God privately, but the world would regard us as strange if we spoke it publicly with reverence."

I like that song from the musical West Side Story in which a young boy falls in love with a young girl, and as he reminisces about her loveliness, he sings, "Maria, Maria, say it loud and there's music playing, say it soft and it's almost like praying." In his love he is hallowing the name of Maria. Would that we could hallow the name of God with such devotion!

To hallow God's name is to treat it with reverence. And what is reverence? It is an inward something. It is a discerning of the highest and the best. It is an approval of that which is of genuine worth. It is the emotion that is stirred within us by whatsoever is pure, lovely and of good report. Of course, it is far more than this. To reverence means to honor. To reverence is to love with a love that is somehow mingled with fear. When directed toward God, it is all of these – honor, love and fear –magnified to a superlative degree.

The first petition, then, is for the hallowing of God's Name. Two ideas are here implied, both of which we meet constantly in Jewish thought. On the one hand, God Himself hallows His Name, makes it clear that He is above this world. The Old Testament is inspired with the sense of the majesty of God, apparent in everything He has made and done. "The heavens declare the glory of God." He speaks to us in the works of nature, in the marvelous events which happened in ancient times and are happening still.

"Holy, holy, holy is the Lord of hosts; the whole earth is full of His glory." But our eyes are so blinded that we cannot perceive His glory. Jesus desires in His prayer, therefore, that our dull senses may be made alive to the Divine presence which is over the world and is ever manifesting itself.

On the other hand, God is hallowed through His people.

This also is an idea which pervades Jewish thought. God had chosen Israel in order that this nation should make Him known to all the earth as the sovereign God. "Be ye holy for I am holy." This verse in Leviticus was singled out by later teachers as the very cornerstone of their religion. Israel was the people of God, Who was the Holy One, separate from all evil, and Israel must keep itself apart, ordering its ways in all things by His commandments.

In our day, as His children, we recognize that God the Father is great and wise and holy beyond our hymns of finest praise and every thought of Him should be reverent. His Name is to be treated as Holy, set apart, sacred. Consequently, we must be careful, lest presuming upon His Fatherhood, we forget to be reverent.

Second, notice that the emphasis is not on the word "hallow: but on "NAME". The mood of the prayer is not a vague reverie, but the worship of God whose nature is reflected in His Name.

I have a friend who was going through a difficult time. He told me in all sincerity that when he prayed the Lord's Prayer, he modified the first line to say, "Our Father, who art in heaven, Harold be thy name." He said he did that because he wanted to feel closer to God as a friend. That's all right, for him. But, to me, that's still just a bit too cozy with the Almighty, and it forgets that we are to hold His name with reverence.

In our day, as God's children, we recognize that God, the Father, is mighty and wise and holy beyond our finest hymns, beyond our highest praise and every thought of Him, therefore, is to be reverent. His name is to be treated as holy, set apart, sacred, special. Consequently, we must be careful, lest presuming upon His Fatherhood, we forget to be reverent.

We have a son and daughter-in-law who spent a lot of time

trying to think up the right name for their new son. "What shall we call him?" Names are important. A man named Harry Lillis, who wanted to be a great pop singer, knew that people wouldn't say, "Let's go out and hear Harry Lillis tonight." Or, "Did you ever hear Harry Lillis singing, 'I'm Dreaming of a White Christmas?'" So he changed his name to Bing Crosby, instead. A man who aspired to be a matinee idol had the name of Archibald Alexander Leach. But, assuming a man named Leach would not be popular, he called himself Cary Grant.

We ask, "What's in a name?" There is something in it, or people would not choose one name rather than another, or wish to change their name.

My own surname, "Palmer" as an example, goes back to the time when Western Europeans were taking part in the Crusades between the 11th and 13th centuries. When they returned from the Holy Land to their homes they placed palm branches in their hats which served as sacred emblems of their visit to Jerusalem. They wanted to signify that they had "walked where Jesus walked." Consequently, these pilgrims were called, "Palmers."

This, however, has nothing personally to do with me, since my Swedish grandfather, whose name was "Johanson," found after his immigration to Chicago that the large number of Johansons in the neighborhood was confusing. So, walking past the "Palmer House" hotel one day, he spied the marquee; he liked the sound and changed his name to Palmer.

The Bible is a book of names, each of which has a meaning. A man's name, in many cases, served not only to distinguish him from his neighbors, but also to give information concerning his character or career. Jacob (The Supplanter) is renamed Israel (Striver with God) to indicate that he has striven with God. Joseph, who was betrothed to Mary, is told, "She shall bring forth a Son; and thou shall call His name Jesus (Jehovah-is-salvation): for He shall save His people from their sins." And in ancient Hebrew usage the name of God signified the revealed character of God. One might say, "Let us appeal to the justice and mercy of God;" or with the same thought in mind, one might say, "Let us call upon the name of the Lord."

Thus, to pray, "Hallowed be Thy Name, is to pray that God may be known as One Who is our Father, Whose nature is holy love, and that, so known, He may everywhere be revered. To pray, "Hallowed be Thy Name," means "Reveal Thyself to me, O God." Long ago Job asked, "Canst thou by searching find out God?" The answer is "no." Man can know God only as God chooses to reveal Himself.

Oliver Wendell Holmes, the distinguished jurisprudent, once said, "I have in my soul a flower called reverence which I must nourish and water at least once a week, and that's why I go to church." God is hallowed through our hallowing His name and realizing we are His people.

"At the name of Jesus every knee shall bow, every tongue confess him Lord of glory now." Do we believe that? "Take the name of Jesus with you, it will guide and comfort you." We don't know what it means to hallow the name of God, and so the translators of new versions of the Bible use the words "respect," "reverence" and "make holy." We can say with Rodney Dangerfield. "God just don't get no respect anymore." To hallow God's name is to be reverent about the Almighty. It is an inward something, a mystery, a sense of wonder, a discerning of the highest and the best, an awesomeness.

A father said to his young daughter: "There's one word I don't want you to keep using so much." She replied, "What word is that, dad?" "Awesome." We don't even realize what is truly awesome in this life. The first petition, then, is realizing that God's name is awesome.

Walter de la Mare asks the question that we all sometimes ask. As he prays, he wonders, "Who is out there?" Before you can pray you must know there is somebody to hear and be conscious of His presence.

God's Name stands for Who He is and What He is. It represents the revelation of The One Eternal Creator God. It includes all means by which He makes Himself known. To the patriarchs, God is the Mighty One, to the children of Israel, He was the great Jehovah; to us who know Him in Jesus Christ, He is "Our Father."

Third, notice that we pray, "Hallowed be THY Name." The mood is not one of selfishness, but of adoring and glorifying the name of God our Father.

We smile at the child who, visiting Boston and having her prayers heard by her hostess, said, "Cabot, be Thy Name." On being asked why she so garbled the prayer, she answered, "At home we are all Halliwells, and pray, 'Halliwell be Thy Name.' Since you are all Cabots, I thought it would be only polite to change the name."

This is precisely the point, however. Much of the problem with many of us in most of our praying is that we pray to a God we have made in our own image, one who we frantically hope bears our name. That is, we hope God stands for the security, the privilege, the desire for which our name stands, a God who will ally Himself with us and with all that is properly designated as ours. Most of us really pray as the first petition, spoken or unspoken, "Hallowed is my name." Do not let anything contrary happen to me or mine, or to my group, or to my purposes. Jesus is saying, on the other hand, "When you get down to the business of praying, the first petition you must utter is 'Hallowed be Thy Name.'"Our young son was saying his prayers one night, and concluded with the words: "God bless Daddy and Mommy, and all my friends, but not the bad guys. Amen."

This petition of the Lord's Prayer, however, reminds us that we must pray for the "bad guys" as well as the "good guys," for it is God's Name, not our own that we are striving to glorify.

Creative power in the world always proves to be destructive when it is used for our selfish purposes. This is true notably of atomic energy. When a scientist works with atomic energy he works with it behind three foot lead walls and with intricate mechanisms so that he never touches the material himself. A man cannot play with atomic energy the way he can move his various trinkets around to suit himself, and we cannot do that with God, either. You dare not make God the instrument of your selfish purposes. He is hallowed and it is not to be confused with your name which you insist upon attaching to everything that comes within your compass.

Prayer therefore involves at the very outset what Paul spoke of as crucifixion—the crucifixion of the self. Plato uttered the same sentiment, "You are created for the sake of the whole, and not the whole for the sake of you." Christians can transfer this thought into their own relationship to God: "We are created for God's sake, for His Name. He does not exist for our sakes or to glorify our names."

Jesus once confronted a crisis in His own life. There came the hour when He had to ask Himself, searching His own soul, "Father, what shall I say?" He was asking, in other words, "How shall I pray? Shall I say, 'Save Me from this hour?'" His enemies had come to Him, you see – bitter persecution was arising from His own people. How easy it would have been to settle for this – forget everybody else. "What shall I say, how shall I pray? Father, save me from this hour! But for this cause came I unto this hour; Father, glorify Thy Name!" And a Voice came from heaven saying, "I have both glorified it and I will glorify it again." What does it mean to be a Christian? It means to give up my name, our names, all of the selfish connotations of our names, and accept the Name of God Incarnate in Jesus Christ.

There is an amusing story of a woman who was questioning the caretaker of a cemetery in Brooklyn. She was hunting for her former husband's grave, and he was not able to locate it. She said, "Well, I don't understand that; his name was John Anderson. Have you looked this up carefully?" "Yes," the director replied, "we have looked it up, and there is no John Anderson. We do have an Elizabeth Anderson, though." "Oh" she said, "that's him. You see, everything is in my name."

May I suggest without irreverence that it is precisely in this spirit that we so often approach the throne of grace —"Everything's in my name." Jesus said, "When you pray, pray like this: 'Our Father, Who art in heaven, hallowed be THY Name.'"

Two centuries ago and even more recently, a belief in witches was quite common in New England. One of the superstitions about witches was that they recited the Lord's Prayer backwards. That was supposed to be a blasphemous thing to do, and brought a punishment with it. No one I know recites the Lord's Prayer backwards today. But many people do turn the prayer around and use it for backward purposes in their practical life. That is, they put their own needs first; their desires come before the worship of God. Many people think first, "Give us this day our daily bread," before they say, "Our Father, hallowed be Thy Name." They want God's will to coincide with their will, God's kingdom to be a reflection of their plans and God's forgiveness to be on their own terms.

Jesus confronted a crisis in his life when came that hour when he had to ask himself, searching his own soul: "What shall I say, Father, save me from this hour but for this cause I have come into the world, therefore glorify thy name in me." And a voice came from heaven, saying: "I have both glorified my name and I will glorify thy name."

A few years ago I walked through the streets of Coventry and approached that charred, bombed-out shell of a cathedral that Hitler had incinerated with his bombs. There's nothing left but a shell today, and inside a charred altar and a burned cross with one word "Forgive." There's a new sanctuary next door but that didn't interest me as much as the remains of the old one. The old one has a number of alcoves, and in each alcove there's a plaque, and on the plaque there are engraved the words: "Hallowed be Thy name;" and then a prayer for some area of life that needs to be made holy. Here are the inscriptions as I wrote them down:

"Hallowed be thy name in education.
        God be in my mind and in my growing."
"Hallowed be thy name in the home.
        God be in my heart and in my loving."
"Hallowed be thy name in recreation.
        God be in my limbs and in my leisure."
"Hallowed be thy name in commerce.
        God be at my desk and at my trading."
"Hallowed be thy name in government.
        God be in my plans and my deciding."

The proper name of God is "our Father" – a name which we hallow by putting Him first and by learning to live as God's children. To look upon our world with any awareness of its tragedy and peril, to reflect upon the pride, greed, and love of power that have brought the world to its present condition, is to realize that one must think and act like a child of God. In our own strength we cannot hallow God's Name. The undertaking is far too great for us. But with God's help we can become His sons and daughters in the sense of caring as He cares for human beings and of making evident in our relationships with others the justice and loving kindness of God.

This prayer then means: Our Father, cause Your eternal nature, revealed in Christ, to be hallowed by us and by all men. This is properly the first petition. We pray it before we pray for the coming of the Kingdom, inasmuch as that coming is for the honor of God's nature; and before we pray for daily bread, for we misuse daily bread if God is not glorified; and even before we pray for pardon, for the pardon must be understood as the gift of Holy Love. We pray this petition first, because God must come first with us if we would live as His own children.

Prayer: *O Lord, give to us a reverent mind when we think of Thee and of all things that tell of Thy glory, so that we may be kept from small and foolish thoughts and may grow in the wisdom revealed through Jesus Christ. Amen.*

WHAT TO SAY WHEN WE PRAY:

4

God Calls You Into Partnership

A newspaper editor, proud of his skill at condensing news articles, boasted that he could reduce the length of the Lord's Prayer. No doubt he could! For many people in their prayers cut out the phrase "Thy kingdom come," since they are in such a hurry to arrive at the petition: "Give us this day our daily bread."

Our desire to diminish the dimensions of the Lord's Prayer is also illustrated by a machine I once saw which engraved the Lord's Prayer on the face of a penny.

While the Lord's Prayer can be reduced to something so small, its scope is large enough to encompass the world as we recall when we pray: "Thy Kingdom come …"

The idea of the Kingdom is the glorious and thrilling, world-shaking and world-transforming truth which Jesus Christ came to bring. Over one hundred times in the Gospels he refers to the Kingdom of God or the Kingdom of Heaven in somewhat synonymous terms.

Jesus said the Kingdom represents God's sovereign rule in heaven and throughout eternity. But also, the Kingdom comes on earth as men and women live more and more under divine constraint of God's will. The Kingdom of God is the rule of

God's Spirit in the lives of those who, by faith and obedience, recognize themselves to be subjects of the King of Kings.

Since the Jews were often afraid of mispronouncing the name of God, as the second commandment told them, "Thou shalt not take the name of the Lord Thy God in vain," they played it safe by not mentioning the name of God, but instead replaced the name of the place wherein he dwells. So, in Jewish theology, we would often read, instead of God's name, heaven, so we talk about the Kingdom, not only of God, but of Heaven as well. The reign, the rule, the Kingdom of God.

In an art gallery, a group of visitors were viewing a painting of a former king of Great Britain. There he was, with his robes of office and his symbols of state. Someone said, "What is he doing?" And the answer was, "Doing? Why nothing, he is just reigning!"

Jesus Christ, in coming to earth, put an end to this type of thinking about a God who is seated in heaven simply reigning. Over one hundred times in the Gospels, Jesus pointed out that God not only reigns over the world, but says Jesus, He seeks to reign in the hearts of people. "The Kingdom of God is within you."

What, then, are some of the implications in praying: "Thy Kingdom come?"

First, when we pray "Thy Kingdom Come," we confess that the Kingdom has not fully come. Wars and rumors of wars, turmoil without and anxiety within, remind us that we live in a world that is in large measure in rebellion against God.

An evidence of this is that even when we pray, "Thy Kingdom come," I do not think we really mean it. We do not like authority, nor will we give in easily even if God is the

King of heaven. We resent this rule and we rage at the way life sometimes treats us.

Charles Colson has a book called Kingdoms in Conflict and it strikes me that this is what we are facing. We sense there is such a thing as a Kingdom of God, Jesus talked about it, and yet it's not really here yet. Now and again when I go jogging I take a Walkman with me, and I place a cassette on the little box in my pocket, and put the earphones over my head, and as I am out jogging, I know there is noise from automobiles and the blare of horns, and people shouting and traffic, and the riveting of a hammer, but I don't really hear that so much because, in my head, I'm hearing Pachelbel's "Canon in D" and I know that there's another kingdom in this world than the kingdom of noise.

C.S. Lewis has, among his books, a clever volume called "The Screwtape Letters" in which he tells of Satan advising his nephew Wormwood on how to distract and destroy people so they will not become Christian. One bit of advice he has for him, as far as the Kingdom is concerned, is: "If someone is sitting in church and they are beginning to respond to the spirit of worship, and being caught up in the idea of Jesus Christ, just whisper in their ear, I wonder what is for lunch today?' 'Did you hear that car horn outside?' Distract them so they will not realize that they are a part of the Kingdom of God at the very same moment they're a part of the kingdom of this world." What it's like, in other words, in terms of the law courts, is that there is a kingdom du jour and a kingdom de facto. Christ has claimed this world but, in fact, we have not all responded to it fully as we might.

The headlines and news broadcasts of any day are enough to convince us that things are not what they should be. Anyone who is at all thoughtful must realize that the world that now is—with its sins and its tragedies is certainly not the world God wants it to be. And so Jesus bids us pray, "Thy Kingdom come."

Many of us on the television look for the daily stock quotations from the Dow Jones. I wish, at times, that there were stock quotations on the Kingdom of Heaven so that we might read, "Peace is up four and one-half points because of the Mid-East peace accord talks." "Security is down six on the notice that people are buying more guns and carrying them to school these days. "Justice lost a point and one-half on the notice that recently juries have not been able to make up their minds between truth and falsehood."

Second, when we pray this prayer, we assert that the Kingdom is going to come. When Jesus turned aside from his carpenter shop one day and set out to make God King over all people and in every department of life, he was certainly undertaking the most difficult task of which we can conceive. But he believed it was a possible task. It was this conviction that gave him his dauntless confidence. And when we pray we are to hold the same high expectation.

Sometimes children see this truth more clearly than do adults. A Sunday School teacher was telling the dramatic story of Abraham and his proposed sacrifice of Isaac. Suddenly a nervous little girl said, "Oh stop—the story is terrible." A little boy exclaimed, "Oh Mary, don't be silly. This is one of God's stories and they always come out all right." As naive as this sounds, it is a child's way of stating a basic truth concerning the coming of the Kingdom of God.

How, then, will the final Kingdom come? There is no doubt as to that when we turn to Scriptures. It will come when the King Himself comes. It will come by another great Divine intervention in human affairs. Christ came once in the "fullness of time" to save sinners. Likewise, in the "fullness of time" he will come again to usher in the glorious Kingdom of God.

In Scotland, during the days of the flight and exile of Prince Charles, the Highlanders never met one another on the wind-swept moors, in a lonely glen, or at the table of a friend, without lifting a cup to the return of their prince and king. The Christian believer ever lifts his cup in faith and hope and love to the return of his Prince and King, the King of kings and Lord of lords. Every time we celebrate the Lord's Supper, that is what we do—"Ye do show the Lord's death till He come." Therefore, he who prays sincerely, "Thy Kingdom come," must also pray that last prayer of the Bible, "Even so, come, Lord Jesus."

Whatever else that mighty second advent hope that glowed and blazed in Jesus' soul may mean, we know that at least it means this—that when man has done everything that he can do to build the everlasting Kingdom, it is God, and God alone, who can make that Kingdom perfect; that somehow and somewhere, in ways beyond our present comprehension, God is going to come breaking in triumphantly; that the age-long warfare between good and evil is not to drag on and on indefinitely as an indecisive warfare, but that one day it is going to end, and end in the victory of God, and in that day the last enemy will be dead beneath Christ's feet forever.

In the third place, we must also realize that the Kingdom has already come. It has been coming ever since the day that God said: "Let us make man." Some sincere Christians believe the Kingdom of God is only in "the sweet by and by." The

Oxford dictionary in commenting upon the vernacular phrase "Thy Kingdom come" says: "Heaven, an echo of the phrase 'Thy Kingdom come' in the Lord's Prayer." But the Kingdom of God means more than this.

The Kingdom came uniquely when Jesus of Nazareth appeared among men. It came in the truth that He revealed. It came in the love that He made manifest. It came in the power that worked through Him, by which the blind were made to see and the deaf to hear and the lame to walk and the poor had good news brought to them, and the sinful and despairing were lifted up into a new life and hope. This power is not in the world, available to all men and able to save to the utmost. "The Kingdom is at hand."

If someone asks, "Where is the Kingdom of God today?" here is the answer: It is wherever a man or woman has made Christ the Lord of life and accepted the rule of God in the heart. Wherever there is right instead of wrong, light instead of darkness, understanding instead of suspicion, love instead of hatred—there is the Kingdom. The Kingdom is a present reality, a partnership, in which every Christian can say, "The King and I," and mean it.

The test of this prayer, "Thy Kingdom come," then, is whether we can pray it in the sense that the Kingdom of God is already in our hearts. Can you pray it in that way? Have you entered into the Kingdom of God through faith? Do you love His Kingdom more or His world more? Are you serving the world more, or are you serving His Kingdom more?

Some time ago, I was in a men's tennis foursome. The four of us were better than average players and we would get together once a week for an hour and a half and play as strenuous tennis as we could. We would often double fault and make our mistakes, but, now and again, there'd be a serve, right down the line, and then a brilliant return, and then a magnificent volley in which everyone was just doing the right thing. Then, finally, maybe I'd be fortunate enough to have a cross court kill and the point would be made, but I would jump up in the air and shout, "That's tennis!" What had I been doing the other hour and a half—was that tennis, too? Sure. But now and again it goes just right, and things are working the way they're supposed to be working.

I look into the lives of the people around me and I see a young student, studying during the day, working every night, striving for a career of service and I say that's the Kingdom. I see a doctor, saying, "I cannot heal anyone. I can just, by the grace of God, provide those conditions under which the Great Physician can heal." And healing comes, and I say that's the Kingdom. Or, I see a man rising for work, coming home at the end of the day, laboring at a task he doesn't really enjoy in order to provide enough that his family may be fed and clothed and housed, and his children educated, and I look at him and I say there's the Kingdom. Or, I look at an older woman, who has lost her family and is living all alone, but she comes to church each Sunday morning and occupies her special place, and she tells me, "I pray for you and this church every day, and if there's anything I can do from my home, I will be glad to do it." She has a kind and gentle word and a smile for anyone she sees, and I say there is the Kingdom of God.

If someone asks you today where the Kingdom of God is now, I have an answer. It is wherever a man or a woman or a young person has made Jesus Christ Lord, and accepted him as Savior, and has determined that they are going to be partners with him in making his love and his life and his kindness and his goodness and his grace known among those with whom they come in contact. Wherever there is right instead of wrong, and love instead of hatred and peace instead of war, there is the Kingdom of God. The Kingdom of God is a present reality, it is a partnership into which you and I enter daily with our God, so that we can say, "It is the King and I living this life."

Jesus said, "The Kingdom of God is within you." The minute a man begins honestly to pray this, he moves from comprehension to commitment. He really is saying, "Thy Kingdom come in me." It will then have all sorts of repercussions. By definition, the Kingdom is a relationship; it is not established by geographical boundaries; it is not characterized by departments. To have a Kingdom you must have a King and you must have people who are subject in loyalty and obedience to the King. The Kingdom of God is the relationship between men who have accepted in their minds and hearts the sovereignty of God for them; who are trying to commit themselves more completely to this sovereignty through prayer; and who are further trying to exemplify this sovereign relationship in their attitudes toward their fellow men.

Fourth, when we pray, "Thy Kingdom come," we are committing ourselves to the task of furthering the Kingdom. If anything is to be done toward furthering the Kingdom in this generation, you and I are the ones who must do it. And yet, I suspect most of us are fearful about the coming of the Kingdom for it would mean reordering our lives in ways we fear would be too painful. Unless we are in the depths we're generally satisfied with things the way they are.

Thomas Carlyle said, "Make of yourself an honest man

and there will be at least one less rascal in this world." Robert
Frost brought it up to date when he said, "Get ready for the
one-man revolution. It's the only revolution that ever comes
to this world." That is a difference that one person can make,
and you can say that you will put the stubborn ounces of my
weight on the side of God and goodness and love, instead of
on the Devil's side.

Some time ago I spoke at a supper on one of my Oxford
teachers, C.S. Lewis. Then we all went to see the film about a
portion of his life called Shadowlands. It set me to thinking.
Before I ever knew who he was I had read C.S. Lewis in college
and in seminary, but, very frankly, I wasn't attracted to him,
too simplistic, I thought. Then I had the privilege of sitting
at his feet and hearing the cadence of his lines, and seeing the
warmth in his face, and the love in his eyes and the brilliance
of his personality, and the graciousness of his ways, and I fell
in love with him. I, suddenly, for the first time, heard C.S.
Lewis. The mechanics I had known before, now I heard the
music. And the wonder and the mystery of it came across to
me. Yet, I'm still searching for C.S. Lewis. I was reading him
again this last week, and coming across phrases that thrilled
me and brought me to new understandings of truth. Because
he was once with me I now want to follow his teachings into
the future.

The Kingdom once came with Jesus. The Kingdom is
still to come, but you wouldn't be praying for the Kingdom
now if it hadn't come for you at least once in some experience,
in some insight, in some truth, in some presence, so that you
say something like, Oh, I know Jesus once came 2,000 years
ago, and I hope and pray he will come again, but I can do this
because he came for me in my life and gave me the power to go

on and the strength to overcome and the love to endure. I've had a taste of the Kingdom because I've met the King. That's what makes the Kingdom worthwhile, my friends.

That's why one question leaps out of the scriptures for me; one challenging word comes out of each of the gospel stories which no living soul can possibly avoid. Is Jesus Christ the Lord of my life? Is he King of the domain for which I have a concern? Think what would happen if each and every member of your Church could so surrender their lives to Christ that all could say, "May the Kingdom come in me, may the Kingdom come through us, may the Kingdom come between us here and now! This is what generated that magnificent vision of a day when heaven itself will ring with the mighty tumult of voices, and their adoring, rejoicing cry shall be "the Kingdom of God is come, and of our Christ, forever."

Isn't this what we sing about at Easter and, sometimes, at Christmastime? Isn't this what inspired Handel to write the "Messiah?" There's a particular passage in the "Messiah" that I love. It's that part where we read, "The Kingdom of this world is become" –and the musical notation is pianissimo, sing it subdued and quietly. Right after that there is a fortissimo, and the basses are to rise up and sing one octave higher and the sopranos an octave and a third higher, and it comes out "the Kingdom of this world is become the Kingdom of our Lord and of His Christ, and He shall reign forever and ever." Handel was right when he wrote it that way. There is the contrast between the kingdom of this world and the Kingdom of our Christ, between the kingdom around us and the Kingdom within us. It is for this Kingdom within that we pray.

There are some who contend that it is all out of our hands and that man and woman have no responsibility for the establishment of God's Kingdom on earth. They say that God's Kingdom is wholly miraculous and entirely dependent upon the sovereign action of God. This view has been taken by many of Europe's theologians following the Second World War, and is shared by many in this country as well. This view seems to recur especially in periods of great stress. It can serve as a warning to Americans lest we make the mistake of confusing man's progress with God's purpose, and identifying our prosperity with God's providence.

Ralph Waldo Emerson once said, "We have improved means to unimproved ends." So man's monuments span the rivers, cross the continents, and pierce the skies. But I do not believe in them. A snowflake is a monument to winter, but it melts away. A teardrop is a monument to sorrow, but it dries up. And so does man's progress. Yet so many have obscured the Kingdom of God by their private causes. "God the Father, Son and Holy Ghost," has been rapidly replaced by a new trinity entitled, "Food, clothing and shelter." The new utensils of faith become the broom that makes the clean sweep, the soap for the skin you love to touch, and the automobile that makes you the envy of the neighborhood.

The Kingdom of God becomes a reality, however, not through our own wisdom and strength, but through our obedience to God. Such obedience makes discipleship with Christ possible, and the disciples, experiencing the high calling of God in Christ, become "the salt of the earth" and "the light of the world." They are the leaven of society, bearing in their own lives the leaven of the Kingdom of God. Here then is the great reason why prayer is so very important. If the Kingdom of God is to come with effectiveness on earth, we must pray, "Thy Kingdom come on earth as it is in heaven."

Augustine once prayed, "Lord, make me pure, but not yet." We pray, "Thy Kingdom come, but not now, not here, and certainly not in me." We like to look down our noses at people in whose lives the Kingdom seemingly has not come. Yet what was it that Jesus said to many "religious" people of His day, "The publicans and prostitutes will go into the Kingdom of Heaven before you." What did He mean? He meant that the publicans and prostitutes are at least so overwhelmed with the sense of their own inadequacy and their own sin that they know they must pray for God's grace. They know they are not going to do anything in and of themselves, and so they pray, "Thy Kingdom come."

One question leaps out at us from every page of the gospels, one challenge which no soul can avoid: Is He the King of my life? Think what would happen if each and every one of us completely surrendered his life to Christ as King. Think what it would mean for us. Think what it would mean for the world around.

Dwight L. Moody, the evangelist, once claimed: "The world has yet to discover what God can do with one life that is totally committed to Him."

During World War II a young man was discussing his ideals with some friends, one of whom retorted, "But you must be realistic. These things of which you are speaking are the laws of the Kingdom of God, and it hasn't come yet." The young man responded, "I recognize that it has not come for you, nor for the world; but the Kingdom of God has come for me."

Can we say the same? The Kingdom of God comes whenever and wherever the justice, the mercy and the love of God is expressed in human life.

In other words, the Kingdom of God isn't some external circumstance, but an internal conviction. How then does God change the world? By changing you! His monuments are men. For no rearrangements of bad eggs can make a good omelet. It is the heart of man that counts.

What after all is history? Is it the cold, impartial record of events, or is it heated by the warm biographies of people? Who can recall the party ticket Lincoln ran upon? Or who can name the war when Florence Nightingale began her work? History is people.

So the kingdom comes in our world through people. This means that you and I need to be what God intends us to be. For as John wrote, "Beloved, we are the children of the Lord." Paul said, "We have this treasure in earthen vessels, always bearing about in our body the dying of our Lord Jesus Christ."

Napoleon was en route as he retreated through the Russian winter. Marshall Ney had volunteered to lead the rear guard left behind to cover tracks. It was a bloody business and it meant almost certain death. The army did come through, and sometime later, while the officers were eating in a tent; a blood encrusted soldier fell inside. They asked, "Who are you?" "I'm Marshall Ney!" They stared in unbelief. "Where is the rear guard?" And he pulled himself up to his full height and spoke deliberately, "I am the rear guard." And you are to be God's Kingdom, wherever you are. So, when you kneel down to pray, "Thy Kingdom come," include the overture, "O Lord, beginning now, with me!"

These are the things we need to remember when we pray, "Thy Kingdom come." Though it has not fully come, it shall come some day when Christ returns. Meanwhile, let us be thankful for the evidences of His Kingdom already in the world, and dedicate ourselves to the furtherance of this Kingdom.

For me, the prayer, "Thy Kingdom come" means something like this: "Lord Jesus, come my way. Give me wisdom, give me the wish, give me the will not to have it my way, but to do it your way, to do what you want, not what I want. I want to be secure: You call me to venture in faith; I want all that money can buy. You want to give me that which is priceless; I want revenge, and You want forgiveness; I want hatred, and you want love. Help me to go, not my way, but Your way. For, if I don't I've lost my own way. If I do, I am found. When I'm found by You I can somehow find myself and others, and take to others the breath of life that comes by Your Spirit to me from You. So, Lord Jesus, come. Come out of the blue in a surprising, unexpected way, but prepare me to be ready to see and hear and receive that coming. Let me not be slow to reach for the stars, because once the stars fell upon me through that Superstar of all, Jesus Christ, I was forever new."

There was once a great moment in the Roman Senate, when Rome had been humbled on the battlefield by the might of Carthage, and pessimistic voices were counseling surrender. An old senator cried, "Stop!" leaping to his feet. "Remember this—Rome does not go into battle; Rome goes to war!" Remember this, in the fight with your problems, Christ's men and women do not go to battle, merely, they go to war, for right against evil. The King's men refuse to quit the field until every foe is vanquished, knowing that the issues of life and of the world are ultimately in the hand not of all the king's horses or all the king's men—but of the King Himself.

This is the confident note that Jesus struck. Beyond the cross—the open tomb; beyond death—eternal life; beyond our weakness—God's strength. This was the eternal hope He gave the world, signed with His own name and guarantee. This was what generated the great vision of the seer with whose book the New Testament closes, the vision of a day when heaven itself will ring with a mighty tumult of voices, and their adoring, rejoicing cry will be: "The kingdoms of this world are become the Kingdom of our Lord and of his Christ; and He shall reign forever and ever …Even so come, Lord Jesus."

Prayer: *O God, for any way in which we have resented and resisted Thy rule we ask to be forgiven; for any way in which we may further and foster Thy faith we ask to be strengthened, in order that we may become consecrated citizens of Thy Kingdom, revealed through Jesus Christ our King. Amen*

5

How Can You Know The Will of God?

"If I could go to a slot machine, put in a dime, pull a lever, and get a little card telling me just what God wants me to do – I'd do it." That was said recently by someone who was trying to sort out his desires from God's will.

Most of us, at some time, have confused our will with God's will. And so we were not surprised when the movie version of The Ten Commandments was being filmed that there were so many tryouts for "The Voice of God." Most of us make up our own minds and then take these decisions to God in prayer and say, "My will be done."

We are prone to make our petulant demands on God. We keep him well informed of our whims, and we offer him the benefit of our advice. We make a shopping list of personal demands and call it prayer. Someone in Oklahoma even went so far as to announce he was going to assure his football team's victory by prayer. I have no sympathy with that kind of thinking, for in the first place it is plain blasphemy, and in the second place I was cheering for Nebraska.

One of the historians of the Civil War period states that the close relationship between General Lee and the man who was known as "Lee's Right Arm," General "Stonewall" Jackson, lay in this, that Lee was first attracted to Jackson because he did not have to argue with him over strategy or to assuage his own sensitive pride. But God has to spend a great deal of His time "arguing with us over strategy" and "assuaging our sensitive pride."

No wonder, then, that Jesus included this petition in the Lord's Prayer: "Thy will be done on earth, as it is in heaven." When we repeat these words we are asking, in effect, "May there be created here on earth those conditions in which the will of God is done clearly and unmistakably as it is in heaven." In Jesus we see the One in whom this heavenly fulfillment shines as in a mirror! For He alone could utter concerning Himself that tremendous saying, "My food is to do the will of my Father in heaven."

Our understanding of the will of God must be placed within the context of the family if we are to comprehend this petition of the Lord's Prayer, which begins with the words "Our Father." An illustration of this comes from an incident in the Gospel of Matthew when Jesus asked of His disciples, "Who are my mother and my brethren? …. They who do the will of my Father in heaven."

One who tried to do the will of God, certainly, was the Apostle Paul. In his letter to the Colossians, he writes: "I do not cease to pray for you that you may be filled with the knowledge of His will." J.B. Phillips translates this as "seeing things from God's point of view." To see things from God's point of view, I believe, is the key to understanding His will.

Recently, I conducted a survey asking people, "Can you really know the will of God?" and I had a number of different responses from Christians and non-Christians alike. Some declared, "You cannot know, as an insignificant human being, the mind of the Creator of the universe." Others said, "Well, we can know God's will in the big things but not in the small things. Think about that phrase, 'Don't sweat the small stuff,' and it's all small stuff." Others said, "Yes, I think we can know the will of God if we try hard enough. We have the Bible and all we need do is open the Bible and follow what it says."

The problem I have with this is that I have been in Bible study groups with many people where we read the same Scripture. Yet different members of those Bible study groups have come out with entirely different ideas of what God is saying. In other words, it is not just what God is saying, but it is what we are hearing as it applies to our lives, that determines how we understand His will. Someone suggested, "All you have to do is open the Bible...it's like picking up a telephone. Dial the right number, and then listen for God's word for your life." The problem I see with that is, not all of us are attuned to the same language, have good hearing, have an open and receptive attitude, or come from the same place. I was reminded of this by a hot-line direction which was given to me. It says:

- If you are obsessive compulsive, press "1" repeatedly.
- If you are co-dependent, please ask someone else to press "2".
- If you have multiple personalities, please press "3, 4, 5 and 6."
- If you are paranoid-delusional, we already know who you are and what your want: just stay on the line so we can trace the call.
- If you are schizophrenic, listen carefully and a little voice will tell you which number to push.
- If you are manic-depressive, it doesn't matter which number you press, no one will answer you anyway.

And so it depends on who we are and where we are as to what we hear God saying at times, doesn't it?

How can we know the will of God? I suspect this is a prayer which I have offered more in my life, every day that I live, than any other: "May Your will be done in me, O Lord." And our own Lord struggled with this question. You remember in the Garden of Gethsemane when he was facing the cross, he prayed, "May this cup pass from me; nevertheless, Thy will be done." We may pray something of the same prayer, but we reverse those phrases, don't we? We say, "Thy will be done"; nevertheless, I want my will to have priority.

In my own personal pilgrimage, I think I've taken at least one little baby step forward in advancing from "willing" to "wanting" the will of God. When we think of the image of the potter and the clay, if the clay becomes hardened, it is thrown away. For God to continue to work, to mold us, our hearts need to be soft, malleable, willing to be shaped by his loving hands. As I try to understand the will of God for my life and for other people's lives, I hold to three grand truths that we proclaim about God. We say God is all-knowing, we say God is all-loving, and we say God is all-powerful. I submit to you, you can't hold all three of those views and make any sense out of God's will in the world. The key words are, Jesus said, "Pray to God as Father." Now, any father or mother that I know is not all-powerful. God is sovereign, to be sure, but I think that God, in working His will in this world has relinquished, held back, does not choose to exercise, all His power in our lives.

Why? Because he made us not as puppets on a string, but as partners in the kingdom. By giving us will power He has given us "won't" power at the same time. Once we have "won't" power, we not only can fashion His will, we can 'fracture' His will.

When you read the book of Job you come across this same dilemma: God's all-power, God's all-love, God's all-knowing. You can pick two of the three propositions, but you can't have all three at the same time, because God chooses to limit His power in our lives. We are in a world with over six billions of other people, a world in which we choose to spend more on armament than on medical research, and so many diseases still plague us. Many people are apt to harm us, and there are others who are ill in minds that do crazy things in this life. Every time we drive on a road or walk through the streets, our lives are, in a sense, in the way of harm, and God allows accidents to occur the way you and I as parents allow our children to make a mistake or even to be injured.

It is a stiff struggle to go from 'my' will to 'Thy' will, when we pray, 'Thy will be done." Jesus said, "Pray that it may be done on earth, as it is in heaven," not just as it is in heaven, because we know in heaven that the saints and the angels are now doing His will. In the same way that His will is being done there, He wants us to seek to do His will in specific ways on this earth.

Charlie Brown was carrying a placard that read, "Stamp out things." Lucy said, 'Charlie, you've gotta' be more specific." So, he goes out to consider this, and in the last frame of the cartoon strip he's carrying the amended sign: "Help stamp out things that need stamping out."

Jesus becomes very specific about God's will being done. He tells us where God's will is being done on earth: at the table of a money changer in a temple, at the repentance of a prostitute in a crowd, at the joining together of brothers who have been arguing. He tells us where and He tells us how God's will is being done by caring, by loving, by submitting to

God's power on the cross, and by responding to God's life at the grave. We have Christ in His teachings and in His living, pointing the way for us so that we may understand something of the will of God. Thus, when we pray, "Thy will be done," we need not pray in resignation.

When Bill Coffin was Pastor of the Riverside Church in New York City, he lost his son, Alex, in a tragic automobile accident in Boston. He was sitting in his sister's house the next day, still weeping over his son's death, when a well-intended neighbor came in with a casserole. As she looked at Bill, she shook her head and said, "This will of God, sometimes I don't understand it. With that, Bill answered her in righteous indignation, "Was it the will of God that my son Alex should not have checked his brakes? Was it the will of God that Alex had too much to drink that night? Was it the will of God that the Boston Harbor Authority had no guard rail on the portion of the road where the accident occurred? When Alex's car went down into the black waters of Boston Harbor the first person to weep was the Heavenly Father."

God loves us and there are things which happen to us in this life that are not God's will. You say, "Ah, but is not everything God's will?" I have been helped immeasurably by a series of lectures I heard delivered some years ago in London in the St. John's Presbyterian Church by Leslie Weatherhead after his City Temple had been bombed out by the Nazis. The lecture has been published in small book form called The Will of God. I suspect many of you know about it. He makes three simple points, and that's what I have to share with you today.

God's will is being done in this world and you and I can pray for God's will, but when we pray, realize that there is such a thing as the intentional will of God, what He wants. There is such a thing as a circumstantial will of God, the things that happen we don't want to happen. And then there is such a thing as the ultimate will of God, in which He does accomplish his purposes.

What I'm suggesting is that God advises us and we can pray for His advice in our prayers. We have to realize also that God allows us to make mistakes and be hurt; but God also accomplishes his will. It is not the will of our Father in heaven that any should perish: "God so loved the world that He gave His only begotten Son that whosoever believes in Him should not perish but have everlasting life." The one who responds to God's spirit and claims Christ as Lord and repents of sin and puts one's trust in God and accepts His grace—God will not let that one go and His will shall be accomplished, ultimately, in that person's life.

Let us look at these three aspects of God's will, for which we have a right and a responsibility to pray, and if you don't feel some struggle in your conscience when you're praying for the will of God, then I wonder just a little bit about your pilgrimage. Abraham struggled with what it means to covenant with God. Job wrestled with the angel of God, striving to know God's will. David wept bitter tears at the grave of his son asking: "What is your will?" Even our Lord prayed, "Let this cup pass from me. Nevertheless, not my will, but your will be done.

The only two kinds of people I know who don't have this struggle are those who have grown complacent, and there are complacent Christians, who assume that either they can't know the will of God, or they can't know it for sure. If you're not a complacent person, maybe then you are a complete saint. Which are you, a complete saint or a complacent Christian? I'm not either. I'm somewhere in the middle, struggling with what is God's will for my life. So I look at this question and I know, first of all, that God advises us of the way to go. "This is the way, walk ye in it," says the Word. This is God's will in the sense of his ideal intention.

I believe that, for Jesus, this will of God was not just a distant idea, but a present help. When Jesus taught this prayer, he was already submitted to and in touch with the will of God. Further, he taught us this prayer because he believed God's will in the world is the reality with which we must deal. Only too often we are victimized by horizontal thinking as if God's will is something which we will discover in heaven. However, if we would think vertically, we would discover His will is breaking in now whenever our will submits to His will. God's will is not just a decree but a living presence.

I had an experience some years ago with my family. We were cruising on a 48-foot yacht with some friends of ours up the west coast of Florida from Naples. Each evening we would enter some marina, then dock and go ashore for a meal and spend the night there. By the time we arrived in Tampa, I was steering the yacht. As we neared the harbor, it was growing dark and as some of you know, Tampa Bay can be a formidable place. There's a huge harbor-bay bridge, illuminated at night. The starboard side is very rocky. There are ocean-going tankers, cruise ships and a host of smaller pleasure boats. My friend, who owned the ship, suggested, "There's no problem here. You've got the path of the red lights and the green lights. Stay between them and the marina toward which we are headed is marked by that blue beacon and along the walk, leading out from there on the dock are a series of lights. When they are all in alignment, you know you're in the center of the channel."

God has given to every one of us here, His word, His spirit, His church, and with these guidelines, we need to say, "May my will, O Christ, be yours." Like the lights in the channel, in my own life, there are a number of lights that I try to have lined up: my own personal experience, the advice of trusted friends, my feelings about something, what my mind tells me, my reading habits, what I do and feel and think. When these things are in alignment, then I have some assurance I'm somewhere in the center of God's will for my life.

My problem is that when it comes to knowing the will of God, I have 20-20 hindsight. Have you ever had the feeling, "Oh, if I only had said that...?" Or, "I wish I had done that..." There are some times in my life - my conversion experience, my call to the ministry, my marriage decision - when I gave some forethought to, and had some prior understanding of the decisions I was making and their implications, but most of the time I travel by faith, not by sight.

I do not believe that God, intentionally, would pour undeserved misery, disappointment, or ill health on His beloved children, and then ask them to look up through their tears and say, "Thy will be done." We must leave behind us the idea that everything that happens is the will of God in the sense of it being His intention.

When a young missionary declares his readiness to dedicate his life in order to bring the good news about Christ to people who have not heard it, then might we speak of God's will. Not just when a woman is beaten and murdered in her home, but when a crime is prevented, we might say: Thy will be done." Not when a soldier is killed, but when warfare is ended and men of all nations begin together to build a new world, that is the time to say, "Thy will be done." Not just when a baby dies; but when two young people take their little one before the altar to dedicate him to God, that is the time to say, "Thy will be done." What I am stating is that at times we use the phrase "God's will" when the very opposite of God's will is being done.

Someone here says, "Bob, if I want to believe that when the bullet comes, if it's got my name on it, I'm gone; otherwise I don't have to worry." Or, "I believe in fate, or karma, or whatever you call it. What's wrong with that?" I see two things wrong with believing that all things that occur must be God's intended will for my life.

First of all, if you hold a wrong idea and you get into a tough situation, I don't think that wrong idea is going to support you. For example, when we lived in the Pacific Palisades in California, back in the 1950's, many people were afraid that the communists were going to drop an atomic bomb on us any day. I remember even having nightmares about it at the time. People were building bomb shelters. We didn't happen to build one, but some of our neighbors built bomb shelters. Our houses looked out on the Pacific and we didn't want to destroy that view – and in California you can't build a basement— so the bomb shelter was built in the front yard. You could drive along the street where we lived, Enchanted Way, (that's a California address if there ever was one) and here and there would be a bomb shelter, a large concrete bomb shelter, covered over with grass, palm trees and flowers so you wouldn't know for sure what it was, but everybody did, anyway. One of our neighbors didn't have enough money, so he had some plywood painted to look like concrete. Now what's the problem with that? As long as there was no war, there was no problem. But it was built to protect him from a bomb and if a bomb ever fell it would be no good at all. Of what value is an idea that would fall apart at the time of crises?

The second thing I want to say is that, people tell me, "But Bob, things like war and illness bring out the best in us." My friends, I have never seen a fig tree that bears olives, or evil that bears good. "By our fruit we shall be known." If I was to take a needle and scratch my hand and blood came forth, was it the needle that caused the blood? I don't think so. The blood was there all the time; the needle simply revealed the blood. I'll tell you a secret about myself. I love in the sunshine and I learn in the darkness. When things are going well, I'm not apt to learn anything, because I know I've got it made, I'm secure. But when things aren't going well, then I start saying, "Oh God, I'm in trouble again. Teach me, I am ready to learn."

For example, let's suppose you're riding in a 747, and the pilot announces a terrible turbulence and the plane starts rocking—that's when you pray, not when it is smooth flying. This is the way it is with most of us in life, and maybe that's why God does send some troubles to us. Maybe that's why Paul said, in Roman's 8:28: "We know that in all things" not, "all things work together for good. That's not what my Bible says. My Bible reads that "....in all things God can work to bring about good for those who love Him." That's what Joseph discovered in the 50th chapter of Genesis when, after being sold into slavery and finally rising to a position of power, when his brothers came before him he said, "You intended this to be evil, but God made good out of it."

So, my friends, what I'm saying is, God advises us but God also allows us. The circumstantial will of God - God allows us to make mistakes and to be hurt the way you and I allow our children to be hurt. In other words, what we need is a Plan

B for our lives. We all have Plan A, what we want to become and do, but I've often had to live according to my Plan B. I've discovered though, that sometimes the best can come out of second best; sometimes Plan B turns out to be finer than I ever dreamed for myself.

Let's just say, for example, that a husband and wife had noble dreams for their son. The husband was a noted surgeon and he wanted his son to be a surgeon, taking him to his office, encouraging him to enroll in biology class, sending him away to Harvard, and after the first year the boy came home and said, "Dad, I want to be a poet." "A what?" "I'd like to write poetry." That father, in his love, knowledge and power would say, "Son, whatever you are called by God to do, do it to your best." He wouldn't deny his fatherhood, he wouldn't write the child out of his will; he wouldn't say, "You're not my son anymore." The mother and father would stand by that son, and that is the way God is with us. We can make our mistakes, but still God has an unconditional love for us.

Like the story of a certain pulpit nominating committee. They were calling a man to come to their church, and the chairman was becoming anxious that he wasn't receiving an answer from this man to whom a call had been extended, so he telephoned to the minister's home. A young boy answered, and the chairman asked, "Is your dad going to accept our call?" The boy answered, "I don't know. Daddy's downstairs praying but Momma's upstairs packing."

Have you ever felt that tug, should we or shouldn't we? In differing circumstances we're going to question and feel this tug as long as we live, yet we sometimes assume that we know more than God. For instance, in the church that I served in one community, there was an adjacent building with a fine nursery.

WHAT TO SAY WHEN WE PRAY:

In the nursery there was a sign with this quote from Revelation: "We shall not all sleep but we shall all be changed." Let's just say for a moment, that some little kid stood up in his crib, adjusted his three corner pants and said, "I want us to get organized against our folks because they're over in the sanctuary; we have to sleep down here in these cribs while they're up there sleeping in their pews. We have to have Pablum and they've got coffee and donuts. This afternoon we have to take a nap and they're going out golfing. Life isn't fair."

Do you suppose God looks at us like a father loves his children, like a mother comforts her own, and says, "Oh, you kids, you just don't understand." I think that's what happens frankly. Why do we insist on being more than we are? Wasn't that the mistake in the Garden of Eden? They wanted to be like God, so they disobeyed God.

Perhaps childhood's tragedies are to us what our tragedies are to our heavenly Father; not that He is callous any more than the ideal parent is callous, but His perspective is different.

But the thought that can comfort the child, comforts me. If the child thought about it, I think he would say, "There is much I don't understand, but I know that my father loves me and wants the best for me." So, for myself, I am quite certain that because God is love, there is nothing in this world that can be regarded as meaningless torture. There is much I cannot understand. But because I know Him as He is revealed in Jesus, I know that although I cannot understand the answer to my question, there is an answer, and in that I can rest content.

"I only know I cannot drift
Beyond His love and care."

Even Jesus himself did not say, "I have explained the world." What he did say was, "I have overcome the world." If only we can trust where we cannot see, and walk in the light we have, which is often very much like hanging on in the dark. If we do faithfully that which we see to be the will of God in the circumstances which evil thrusts upon us, we can rest our minds in the assurance that the circumstances which God allows, reacted to in faith and courage, can never defeat the purpose which God ultimately wills. So doing, we shall wrest from life something splendid. We shall find peace in our hearts. We shall achieve integration in our minds. We shall be able to serve our fellow men with courage and joy. And one day, we shall look up into Christ's face and understand. Now we see in a mirror, darkly. But then, face to face. As Dante, the Italian poet said, "In His will is our peace."

During a flood in Ohio, a man was sitting on top of his roof. The waters were rising and the man prayed, "Oh, God, save me." A helicopter came by and the pilot called out, "Are you all right down there?" "Yes, I am trusting in God." People in a motorboat came by and asked, "Are you all right?" "Yes, I am trusting in God." After a time the man prayed, "God, where are you? When will you save me?" God replied, "I already sent a helicopter and a motorboat."

Once there was a man who dared God to speak. "Burn the bush like You did for Moses, God, and I will follow You. Collapse the walls like you did for Joshua, God, and I will fight for you. Still the waves like You did on Galilee, God, and I will listen to you." So the man sat by a bush near a wall close to the sea, and God heard the man, so God answered. He sent fire, not for a bush, but for a church alive. He brought down a wall, not of brick, but of sin. He stilled a storm, not of the sea, but of a soul, and waited for the man to respond. God waited, and God waited, but because the man was looking at bushes, not hearts; bricks, not lives; seas and not souls; he decided God had done nothing. Finally he looked to God and asked, "God, have You lost Your Power?" God looked down and said, "Man, have you lost your hearing."

How sensitive and open are we to God's leading? That which He has begun He shall complete within us and we know that in all things, God is working. "Trust in the Lord with all your heart and lean not to your own understanding. In all your ways acknowledge Him and He will direct your paths." We have God's word on it. Life may not always seem fair to you, but God is good, nevertheless.

This can be illustrated from the life of Jesus himself. It was God's intentional will that Jesus should come to reveal God, and win man back to Himself. It was God's circumstantial will that in the events which transpired, Jesus should accept death in such a positive and creative way as to lead to God's ultimate will – namely, the redemption of man, winning man back to God, not in spite of the Cross, but using the Cross as an instrument to reach the goal of God's Ultimate will.

Our daughter, once when she was in junior high school said, "Daddy, tell me I can't go out with Jim unless I come home by 9 o'clock." Then when she went out she could say, "I can't go with you and my daddy says I have to be home at 9 o'clock." I think that sometimes the rules and regulations God gives us are there so that we might be happier in doing His will.

The omnipotence of God does not mean that by a sheer exhibition of His superior might, God can get His own way. If He did, man's freedom would be an illusion and man's moral development would be made impossible. But God does not engage in such saber rattling. When we say that God is omnipotent, we do not mean that nothing can happen unless it's God's intention. We mean that nothing can happen which can finally defeat Him.

Perhaps everyone could raise some question which would be almost impossible to answer concerning God's ultimate will. Maybe you have lost a loved one tragically, or have suffered a terrible illness, or found your highest hopes frustrated. And now you ask, "How can God ever reach in my life His ultimate will?"

I cannot give you a glib answer. Allow me to say one or two things however. On Good Friday eleven men, in the deepest gloom, felt like some of you. They said in their hearts: We trusted Him. It was His will to establish His kingdom. And now evil has taken Him from us. It's the end of everything."

But they were wrong, weren't they? It was only the end of their mistake and the beginning of the most wonderful use of evil which God has ever brought about. And if you give way to despair, you are wrong too. And one day, like them, you will find out how wrong you were and be sadder at your despair than at your loss. For God can be using even your sadness and despair in His plans and enable you to say, "I can do all things through Christ who strengthens me."

Evil can do terrible things to us. The more I read and think the more I believe in the devil. Someone said, "God lets the devil have a long rope these days." Someone else responded, "Yes, but God keeps hold of the end of it for Himself." Rest in this thought about God's ultimate will. "Eye hath not seen, nor ear heard, neither hath it entered into the heart of man to conceive the things that God has prepared for them that love

Him." Trust God. He who began this strange adventure we call human life will also control the end.

God has a purpose in your life, and no higher good can be yours than to find and follow and fulfill that purpose. As Tennyson, the English poet wrote: "Our wills are ours, we know now how; our wills are ours, to make them Thine."

C.S. Lewis, in his remarkable little fantasy about the hereafter called The Great Divorce fancies himself a pilgrim who takes a bus trip from hell to heaven to see whether he would like to settle in heaven. When he gets there, he speaks with a heavenly guide about the people who "missed the bus" to heaven. He asks, "What of the poor ghosts who never get into the bus at all?" And his guide replies, "Everyone who wishes it does. Never fear." There are only two kinds of people in the end, those who say to God, "Thy will be done" and those to whom God says in the end, "Thy will be done."

There is a story, which I hope is true, of Victor Borge in one of his concerts. At this particular concert, just as the house lights went down and the curtains parted, a little boy, no more than eight or nine years of age, got up out of the front row, climbed up on stage and sat down at the Steinway and started playing Chop Sticks. Victor Borge walked out, made a signal to the audience to be quiet, sat down beside the little boy and started playing melodies based on the little boys fingering. When they finished, both Borge and the boy stood up to a standing ovation. You can buy a recording today of Victor Borge's Rhapsody: Based upon A Theme of Chop Sticks. What I submit to you is that with all our imperfections, all our childishness, all our misunderstandings, God can accomplish His will; He can work to bring about something of glory and beauty in us nevertheless.

Perhaps we have come far enough along now to catch the tone of joy and victory in the words: "Thy Will be done on earth, as it is in heaven." These words were not born of resignation or renunciation. No, there is something radiant and shining about them. They are spoken to none other than our Father in heaven. And we can be sure that if we seek His will as it is revealed through the Bible, through prayer, through the Church, through conscience, and through circumstances, this can only bring peace and fulfillment to our lives. For it is the will of Him Who loves us in Jesus Christ and who has promised that with those who love God, everything works for good, and that where His will rules all will be well. So we can pray with confidence, "Thy will be done, on earth, as it is in heaven."

So, my friends, I hope that through thinking together about the will of God, when you pray that prayer tonight, "Our Father who art in heaven…Thy will be done on earth as it is in heaven," there may be an added dimension of meaning as you contemplate how God allows us to do certain things, advises us to do other things, and in all things accomplishes His will in us. It was this kind of confidence in God's will that enabled John Gilmore in the midst of our bloody War Between the States to pen these words, which became a favorite hymn of the Church:

> He leadeth Me, O blessed thought!
> O words with heavenly comfort fraught!
> What e'er I do, where-e'er I be,
> Still 'tis God's hand that leadeth me.

Prayer: *Our loving heavenly Father, Who dost not will that we should walk in darkness, pour the light of Thy Holy Spirit into our minds and hearts that we may discover what is Thy holy will, and walk in those paths Thou would have us to go. For our sake, for the sake of others, and for Jesus' sake, Amen.*

6

Your Shopping List
is Sacred

"Give us this day our daily bread!" These words are a battle cry resounding throughout our troubled world from Berlin to Baghdad. They comprise a clamant cry of millions who hope through revolution or reformation to take bread from the tables of those who have plenty.

"Give us this day our daily bread!" These words are uttered by millions of hungry people who will die tomorrow unless they are able to beg, borrow or steal bread today.

"Give us this day our daily bread!" These words also comprise our prayer as we approach our Father in heaven from whose hands we have freely received. Yet, for many of us, these words mean scarcely more than they did to the little boy, who misunderstanding the words his parents used, prayed, "Give us this day our jelly bread."

I am thankful that Jesus included this phrase concerning our daily bread. I am glad that Jesus told us to speak to Him, not only about spiritual things like the Kingdom of God, but about the affairs of our own lives as well. For if we split life in two - sacred and secular - then God becomes a halfway God who only rules half of life and your minister is stereotyped in gown and pulpit lest he learns what you are really like. When religion is confined to church, then when worship is over God returns to heaven and stays there till next Sunday at eleven o'clock.

In approaching the fifth phrase of the Lord's Prayer, "Give Us This Day Our Daily Bread," we come upon one more instance of God's desire to give and of our encouragement from Jesus to ask. Throughout the gospels there are recurring instances of Jesus responding to people's requests to give bread, health, healing, salvation, life itself.

In our scripture we find such an instance in which Jesus, venturing beyond the boundaries of Israel, into the land of Samaria, on the coast to the northwest, is confronted not by a Jew, but by a Samaritan, who was hated by the Jews. Not by a man, but by a woman, who spoke out of turn, not according to social custom. Nevertheless, he listened, he heard and he responded. Let's see how Matthew tells the story.

"Leaving that place, Jesus withdrew to the region of Tyre and Sidon. A Canaanite woman from that vicinity came to him crying out 'Lord, Son of David, have mercy on me! My daughter is suffering terribly from demon possession.' Jesus did not answer a word. So his disciples came to him and urged him, 'Send her away for she keeps crying after us.' He answered, 'I was sent only to the lost sheep of Israel.' Then the woman came and knelt before him, 'Lord help me' she said. Then, quoting a Jewish Proverb he said, 'It is not right to take the children's bread and toss it to the dogs.' (The word "dog" here is street curs.) And she responded by saying, 'Yes, Lord, but even the dogs (and the word here is puppy dogs) eat the crumbs that fall from their masters' table'. Then Jesus answered, 'Woman, you have great faith. Your request is granted.' And her daughter was healed from that very hour."

Something as basic as bread and water can mean life. And Jesus, here, not only allows but encourages us to ask for something as simple as daily bread. And when we pray this prayer, let us not just trip over this phrase like it didn't count for anything. Like the little kid who said, "Give us this day our jelly bread." He didn't think ahead of time. Man does not live by bread alone, but by peanut butter as well. We all know that.

Let us look at each word of this phrase, to see what we may experience to enrich our prayer life. The very first word is "Give" and I say, "Thank God for that word." Give. Because it means that we can come and make our request known to our Father in heaven. Jesus not only allows but he encourages us to pray for something as simple as daily bread.

Jesus assures us that He is concerned about all that concerns us. He assures us that God is the Father of all our life. He assures us that we can approach Him not only in our Sunday best, but also when our clothes become soiled and our hands calloused and our faces marked with lines of care. By praying for daily bread we realize that the Lord's Prayer can be uttered at the cradle and at the grave, and at every occasion and every moment in between.

Just imagine! Coming before the Lord of the universe and saying, "Give." What an effrontery! But remember this, he is also our Father in heaven, and it is as His children that we say "Give." When we make this prayer it is not a dowdy demand for table scraps, but a ringing affirmation of the ruler-ship of God.

Man, of course, has his role to play in this as is illustrated by the story of the prizefighter who prayed as he entered the ring. Someone asked a minister who was watching the fight, "Will that prayer help him?" The minister replied, "It will if he can fight." Prayer is no substitute for work. I suppose part of our difficulty is that we think of prayer as an other-worldly thing. We expect God to do things magically, when actually what He often does is reinforce the abilities He has already given us.

But prayer is far more than a healthy exercise, more than a gymnastic device of the spirit by which we are enabled to talk to ourselves and hold our own hands in the dark. Prayer is an opportunity for bringing our requests before God. And what request is more basic than the one for bread? All prayer would die on our lips if it were not for bread. And this request for bread sets our whole mundane life within the "Name" and the "Kingdom" and the "Will" of our heavenly Father. This prayer for bread reminds us that we live in a dependence which no human skill or striving can ever change. This truth is not palatable to our pride, but it is still truth.

"Back of the loaf is the snowy flour,
And back of the flour the mill,
And back of the mill is the wheat and the shower,
And the sun and the Father's will."

Life is a table where we wait as children. We are dependent, even though we are allowed to help "our Father" with the chores. Day by day we must pray, "Give us this day our daily bread." Day by day we must thank God for the bread we have already received.

Back in seminary, I read book after book on what can a person pray for; do you pray for the big things, or just the little things? Do you pray for what you want? Jesus says you pray for anything and everything. All our requests are to be brought before God in prayer. Sweet hour of prayer. We are encouraged by Jesus to do this. And what it reminds me of is the fact that this is an honest to God prayer. Up until now we have been praying for His name to be hallowed, to our heavenly father, for his kingdom to come, for his will to be done. Now, we have a new paradigm, something as basic as bread. And it means that we are praying honestly when we ask for something like bread, because we pray for little things in our prayers and we often don't like to admit it. We like to appear that we are so spiritual that our prayers are filled with thanksgiving and love for Jesus. I don't know about your prayer life, but I know about mine. And I will just wager that much of our prayer life is spent in asking for things. I think sometimes we are like the beautiful woman in the Miss America contest. She stands before the television audience and Bob Barker asks, "What do want most of all?"

"World peace."

Like fun, she wants to win the contest.

And we pray for world peace in public, but I'll bet you tonight when you go to bed or tomorrow morning when you arise, you pray for the things that you want.

Now, I will admit, my prayer life changes. When I was a child, I used to pray for a home run when I went up to bat. And I remember when we lived up North, on a cold morning when my old Chevy wouldn't start, I would pray, "Oh, God, let this car start." And it worked.

Since 9/11 I have been praying differently than I did before 9/11. Things like security, freedom from terror. I pray a lot more for our President and the Congress and the armed forces and the intelligence community. I pray more for the safety of our own land. What I am saying is, depending on where we are our prayers take a different form from time to time. But if we are praying honestly to God, then we will admit we are all beggars. Everyone one of us is a beggar. The dictionary says a beggar is someone with a hand out, a suppliant, who is asking for that which he needs and cannot do without. We have homeless people coming to this church every week begging. I am proud of our session for offering a program that gives assistance in the form of food and clothing to people who really need such things.

Depending on who we are and where we are, we have our own scale of needs, don't we? Once bread, water, shelter, clothing are taken care of, then we start praying for other things. I don't know what your prayers are for, but I am thankful that God lets us say "give me." It strikes me that everyday we live we are saying "give" in one form or another. If we go to the Doctor's office we are saying, "Give me health." If we come to the grocery store, we are asking for food. Go to the clothing store, we are asking for a new suit. If we break a wish-bone we are asking for something. If we wish upon a star, we are asking for something. You and I are always asking for things, aren't we?

And Jesus says that is alright. Your heavenly Father knows that you need these things. So go right ahead and ask for them. I think we, in this country especially, need to be aware of the fact that we are already so blessed with so much. When this prayer was uttered originally, it meant that the person offering it was raising his own crops and had to harvest them. He also had to grind the flour. He had to bake the bread. We take these things so for granted.

When we lived in London, we had to go to one store for bread and another store for fish and another store for meat and another store for canned goods and so on. Today you and I have our larders stocked with food already. And even though we pray, "Give Us This Day Our Daily Bread," in the back of our minds we know, we already have it laid away. And we feel pretty smug about that, I suspect. We have access to all kinds of opportunities. When Mikhail Gorbachev came to this country and Ronald Regan showed him through a California supermarket, Gorbachev shook his head and said, "You already have the cold war won, haven't you?"

It's amazing what is available to us. So the point is not simply to go through the motion of praying for bread, but to open the door before our heavenly Father who gives us all things richly to enjoy. Back of the bread is the grain and the flour. Back of the flour is the mill. And back of the mill is the rain and the shower and the love of our Father's will. And so for all the graciousness God grants, He says to us, when you pray, pray for whatever is on your mind and heart, because your Heavenly Father knows already what you need, but He wants you to ask the way a parent appreciates a child's request.

The second word is somewhat threatening to me, because it means I cannot be selfish in my prayers. It is not give "Give me." But "Give us." What I ask for, I must take into account others in the human family. We are not only bakers of bread, we are breakers of bread and we are brothers and sisters in eating that bread. And what happens to us has an influence on others. The whole family of God is in the bread line. So when we pray, "Give us this day our daily bread." We are asking for bread, not only for ourselves but also for others.

I heard someone once say, "I am very fond of the human

race. All my family has belonged to it, and some of my wife's family, too." Seriously, though, God is saying, and life is saying, "You must join the human race. You must not only pray for your bread but for our bread, and for everyone's bread." Here is a reminder that humankind is a family. As if we needed a reminder, for what goes on in one part of our world dramatically affects the rest of the world. Our world-wide family is so interrelated that stocks rise or fall according to what is said in Mandalay or Moscow, and men dear to us are risking their lives in faraway places whose strange sounding names were forgotten the day after we passed our geography test in high school. Social righteousness then is, in a sense, a matter of table manners, and we must ask whether we can afford to glut ourselves while others are hungry.

In a modern play by Archibald MacLeish titled, Panic, a woman who was watching a news bulletin which told of forthcoming depression and unemployment, cried out, "Forgive us our daily bread" – and she made no mistake. Isolationism is worse than a political fallacy; it is religious heresy, for if there is but one God, then there is but one family throughout His earth.

Bread is not only to be eaten; it is to be shared. This is what the writer of Ecclesiastes said: "Cast thy bread upon the waters, and in many days it shall return unto thee." The prayer for our daily bread is not merely that this body and soul may be kept together, but that with this body and soul all of us will be able to serve God and help our fellow man. "He who casts his bread on the waters will find it soggy," quipped a modern wit. But the Bible says: "He who casts his bread upon the waters will find it again after many days, and in many ways. He will find it in the gratitude of the needy. He will find it in the peace of his own conscience. He will find it in the final blessing of Him who is the Bread of Life that comes down from Heaven: "I was hungry and ye fed me....Inasmuch as ye have done it unto one of the least of my brethren, you have done it unto me."

We have a mobile in our house hanging from the ceiling, fashioned after one of Alexander Calder's. It is suspended by monofilament line and it has a series of triangle and circles, octagons and squares. When the wind rustles through, it gyrates. But, if you take one of those elements out, the whole thing collapses. Now you and I are related to the rest of the world in our global village. Let the Wall Street stock market drop a few points and they can feel it in Tokyo or London or around the world.

Orson Welles was one of my favorite actors a few years ago and a brilliant producer and director of motion pictures. If you remember during his later years, he became grossly overweight, like one-third of America, and then some. He said, "My doctor told me that I have to stop having these intimate dinners for four unless I invite three other people to share them with me."

Do we really know how to conserve and utilize what God has so richly gifted for us? When I was a child, now and again my mother would serve broccoli. My opinion of broccoli resembles that of the 41st President of the United States. But when I didn't join the clean plate club, and eat my broccoli, her usual retort was, "Robert, think of all those starving Armenians." As if somehow, my eating a piece of broccoli would help some starving Armenian halfway around the world. On the other hand, this morning I was taking a shower and after I finished I was standing in front of the mirror drying myself, and I said to myself, "You know, I should have done more for those starving Armenians."

Mahatma Gandhi said, "The world has enough food for our need, but not enough food for our greed." Half the world not only went to sleep last night hungry, but half the world went to sleep without ever being asked to vote. Half the world rose this morning and realized that one of their children would die before the age of 18. Half the world has no medical care. Half the world makes their own houses out of mud and clay and palm branches and foliage. Half the world walks on their own feet or on a small beast of burden rather than in an automobile. Yes, we live in a world that needs to be reminded that we are one family. And so, if we have the right to say before our heavenly Father, "Give," it strikes me that others have the right to stand before our windows and see all that we have and say, "Help us, by sharing."

One of the good things about Lent is something we call One Great Hour of Sharing. I know of no other single means where we can multiply our concerns for hungry people through agencies like One Great Hour of Sharing, Meals for Millions, World Vision, Denominational Offerings and the like. Lent is not only a time to give up something for ourselves, but to share something in a positive way for other people as well. We have to do our part. It is not just a question of saying "give me," but what does God expect of us, as well? And then that brief phrase tucked in there, "Give Us This Day." You and I want what we want, right now.

There are people who long for the day when maybe they will be able to have a piece of meat or fish or something more substantial than rice, the most common ingredient in the world's diet. Whereas you and I, after Sunday Church, have numerous restaurants where we can have any kind of food we want to eat. If we do not want to bother with a restaurant, we can drive through and get our fast food, or if we don't want to bother with that we can turn on our microwave and have a full meal in a matter of minutes. We eat and we drink more than we realize. I went to a fast food place the other day and they had three sizes of Coca Cola. Large, Extra Large and Giant Size. No medium or small any more. I am amazed that people can drink 36 ounces of Gulp. How they do it, without brain freeze, I do not know. But we continue on our way. I saw as well the fact that, in America, 8% of our families go to the store each day. In Russia, 50% of the families go to the store for food each day. In Palestine, 100% of the families go to the store for food each day. It is the only way they can get by. They cannot store food like you and I.

We pray and sing about the patience of unanswered prayer. And there is something of that to be sure. Sometimes the reason we pray for something and we don't have it, is because it is the wrong thing and God says "NO." Sometimes we pray for something and we just are not ready to receive it. And God says "GROW." Sometimes we pray for things and the time just isn't right for us. And God says "SLOW." Sometimes we pray for something and we are ready and the time is right and the prayer is right and God says "GO." Remember that when your prayers are sometimes answered in different ways and different times than you expect them to be.

And then the third word. "Give us this day our DAILY bread." That word does not appear anywhere else in the Bible other than in the Lord's Prayer. More than that, it does not appear anywhere else in Greek Literature than in this one place. And so for hundreds of years, Christian scholars said,

"What it means is that Christ is the bread of Life we are to pray for." Very spiritual. Some people still think we have such a spiritual religion. We shouldn't talk about material things, but we actually have the most material of religions. And, after that, when the church became more liturgical and settled in, theologians said, "No, what that means is, the bread of the Lord's Table. The Eucharist, the Mass. That is what we should pray for daily."

In more modern times, they came to such ideas as pray for bread that is sufficient for the day, or pray for bread that we need. The first time we were in Palestine, back in the 1950's, they discovered a parchment which was a woman's shopping list. And the shopping list was divided down the middle. On the one half were the things a woman would buy for the long term. What you and I would call canned goods. You don't buy it every day, you buy it if company is coming or you are waiting for a sale before you buy it. On the other side, it was headed with a word meaning the daily list, things like bread or milk or meat. So this prayer is not an elevated prayer of spirituality. It is so basic that we are to pray for the dailies, the stuff that we need from hour to hour and day to day.

We do not pray, "Give us bread for 365 days," but enough bread for today. This teaches us to trust in God. This does not exempt us from labor. "If a man will not work, neither shall he eat." That was the law the Apostle Paul gave to the early Church.

Do you remember in the Old Testament how God sent manna daily to the wandering children of Israel? They tried to hoard some so they would not have to get up early and gather it every day. And what happened? It spoiled. Some things just must be done daily. And what is more, who can tell how much of the disorder, woe and bitterness of the world is due to this human passion of gathering more manna than is necessary for the day, collecting things, disregarding the rights of others, and forgetting God.

The true attitude towards God is one of trust. Worry is perhaps the most universal, the most exhausting, and the most useless sin. There is sound sense in the old quatrain:

> *"Better never trouble trouble*
> *Till trouble troubles you,*
> *For you only make your trouble*
> *Double trouble when you do."*

In London I once visited the home of Thomas Carlyle. There he had built in the top story a vault-like chamber where he was shut off from all noise. But in his neighborhood there was a rooster whose shrill cry penetrated even to this room. Carlyle was greatly annoyed by this and protested to the owner of the rooster. The man told me that his rooster crowed only three times a day and therefore could not be so great an annoyance. "Yes," said Carlyle, "but if you only knew what I suffer waiting for the rooster to crow!"

A great many people sit around waiting for the rooster to crow, and waiting is really worse than the crowing itself! With a radar screen they scan the horizon for troubles that are yet afar off. They forget what Jesus said: "Which of you by taking thought can add a single cubit to his stature? Take, therefore, no anxious thought for the morrow, for the morrow shall take thought for the things of itself. Sufficient unto the day is the evil thereof."

Fourth, remember that it is bread which Jesus teaches

us to ask for from our heavenly Father. Some of the early Church fathers took this petition for daily bread as referring to spiritual or sacramental bread. But in so doing they missed the materialistic element in the gospels. Our Lord was concerned not only for the salvation of men's souls but for the well-being of their bodies. The difficulty comes when we think of bread as nothing but bread, when we forget its spiritual nature. Whole ideologies have come into being around the idea that since men are animals, bread is the thing. The Communists long ago launched a world program on this basis – the concentration of human energy on the problem of bread.

This request for bread is a prayer in behalf of whatever is necessary for the decent maintenance of the life of the body. It means, by inference, shelter and clothing. It is the answer to all that is implied by being hungry and thirsty, naked and homeless. There is no sanction for the theory, held by some religions, in which matter is evil and the body itself is sinful. To this extent the Lord's Prayer states the case for what has been called the religion of healthy-mindedness, as against unnatural asceticism. For the life of me, I do not see how we can achieve such noble detachment, separate our spiritual selves from the rest of ourselves, as some people imply when they say we should not ask God for things. If I want something, I want it all over. If I need something, the desire is a part of me, in my mind, in my heart, in my bones. If my children are in danger, I am going to pray to God for their protection. If I am flat on my back with illness, I am going to ask God to help me to become better. George Buttrick in his book on the subject of prayer has written: "Prayer is as elemental as a cry in the dark. It's the soul's sincere desire. It's what we want with our whole being." And I believe prayer changes things, and through it

God makes things happen.

A teacher asked a boy in class to name three food essentials. He replied, "Breakfast, lunch and supper." This is a good answer. Bread is a basic need of life, and the problem of getting it consumes a major portion of our energy, and links us up with a vast network of divine and human relationships. Through this petition of The Lord's Prayer, Jesus is teaching that wherever we go and whatever we do, God goes with us; and that, behind things, unseen and unrecognized often but everlastingly gracious, there is a loving heart thinking for His people all the time, planning for them, remembering them, arranging wonderful surprises of sheer goodness for them. As Jesus put it, "If ye then, being evil, know how to give good gifts unto your children, how much more shall your Father which is in heaven give good things to them that ask him. Remember when as His children we were taught to pray, "God is great; God is good, let us thank him for this food. By his hand we all are fed; give us Lord our daily bread." That is what we are invited to ask for here.

I went to Publix Supermarket yesterday and in the bakery section I found 12 different kinds of bread for sale. Then I walked through the commercial section and I found over 40 different varieties of bread; packaged, sliced, pumpernickel, rye, white, Wonder, five grains, three grains, seven grains, enriched, non fattening. Amazing! We, who are so sophisticated, wonder why sometimes we don't appreciate the basic things of life. I don't know how many of you go shopping at all.

There was a retirement home nearby and the wife of an older couple sent the husband out to get some things they really liked. Nellie said, "Bill, would you go out and buy me a chocolate milk shake."

"Sure, honey."

"Ahhhhh, make it a chocolate malt, I like that powder in it."

"OK dear."

As Bill was leaving, she said "Make it a giant size, please."

"OK, dear."

"Make sure its chocolate."

"Chocolate."

"And have them put some of those sprinkles on top, OK?"

"OK, sprinkles on the top, OK, got it."

So, he was gone about 45 minutes before. He came back with a Burger King Whopper. Nellie said, "Honey, where are the French Fries to go with it?"

How much do you and I ask for, when by the time we get it, we don't want it, or we don't remember what we wanted in the first place? We have so much stuff around the house that the job is just to keep things from crowding us out of our own home. We who are so blessed need to remember that we have a Heavenly Father who wants to share and we have a right, therefore, to ask. Not in a selfish way, but remembering that we are members of the entire human family, he will supply our needs.

I remember as a high school student in Chicago, on Sunday evenings, we would travel to South State Street. And there we would give our testimonies, and speak and offer our prayers and our songs in the Union Gospel Mission. After we finished with our evangelistic service, an invitation to people was given, and then they would give people bread and soup. Always after. I would sometimes question that, but I don't anymore. Why? Because I think that sometimes we forget that there is something more basic than the bread we eat. And that is the bread of life.

In Luke 4, Jesus said, "If a father is asked for bread, will he give a stone?" The answer of course is, "No." He added, "Man does not live by bread alone, but by every word that proceeds out of the mouth of God," namely Jesus Christ, the Living Word and the love he has for us all.

One final word might be offered here. The request for bread is set against the larger background of the Fatherhood of God. And just as family conditions may limit what an earthly father is willing to do for his children, so our worldwide family cannot always receive all it wants or needs. Remember, we are not bidden to pray for cake, but for bread. Ours is not a "trick or treat" religion by which we approach God with a threat if He does not give us what we want. This prayer does not imply God's everlasting welfare state in which his every child can "freeload" on the universe. The symbol of our faith is not a horn of plenty but an empty cross.

So if and when there is not even enough bread on the table, remember the lesson of Jesus' temptation to turn stones into bread. He refused. Why? Not because He is indifferent to material needs and social conditions. Indeed, He cares far more about these things than any reformer or politician or philanthropist who has ever lived. The whole point is that when, in spite of his passionate love for people, Jesus refused the shortcut of turning stones into bread, it was because he was in the world to win people, not bribe them. Jesus knows there is a hunger in the human heart deeper and stronger and more insistent than the hunger of bread and material things. And it is this deeper hunger, this nameless longing of the soul can be satisfied, not with bread, nor with riches, nor with any material comfort whatsoever, but only with the broken Body of Jesus the Christ. It is this that Christ came to satisfy. The bread he gives is himself, his body broken for you and me – the very Bread of Life. The day will come when you will not know where to turn unless you have already turned to Jesus Christ.

Prayer: *Dear Lord, give us this day such sufficient food as will nourish our hearts, our minds and our bodies. Help us not to fill up our lives with good things to the exclusion of the best – the Bread of Life – Jesus Christ. Amen.*

WHAT TO SAY WHEN WE PRAY:

7

Do You Find It Hard
to Forgive?

I recall a cartoon showing St. Peter at the gates of heaven, telling a man hoping to gain admittance who complained that he had not sinned all that much. "I'm afraid you did my little man, would you like to see the videotape?" One noted preacher warned that judgment day might be nothing more than having to watch a video tape of your life, as you stand there in the presence of God Almighty. It sounds rather scary.

But, most of us don't require a video tape to be reminded of past sins. The glad news of the Gospel, however, is that forgiveness is available. Now is a good time to be asking ourselves questions about our spiritual growth in forgiveness and grace. In this regard, let me share a series of questions that John Wesley and his friends at Oxford asked themselves in their private devotions over 200 years ago. I believe there is food for thought here for each of us as we ponder our need to forgive.

- Am I consciously or unconsciously creating the impression that I am a better person than I really am? In other words, am I a hypocrite?
- Am I honest in all my acts or words, or do I exaggerate?
- Do I confidentially pass on to another what was told to me in confidence?

- Can I be trusted?
- Am I self-conscious, self-pitying or self-justifying?
- Did the Bible live in me today?
- Am I enjoying prayer?
- When did I last speak to somebody else, trying to win that person for Christ?
- Do I disobey God in anything?
- Do I insist upon money I spend?
- Have I done something about which my conscience is uneasy?
- Am I defeating in any part of my life? Am I jealous, impure, critical, irrational, touchy or distrustful?
- Do I thank God that I am not as other people, especially as the Pharisees who despised the publican?
- Is there anybody who I fear, dislike, disown, criticize, hold resentment toward or disregard? If so, what am I doing about it?
- Do I grumble or complain constantly?
- Is Christ real to me?

In my personal prayers, this is the phrase which follows first after addressing our heavenly father: "Forgive my sins."

A Sunday church school teacher was explaining to class the meaning of the phrase in the Lord's Prayer, "Forgive us our debts as we forgive our debtors." He commented that "debts" referred to sins, and asked, "Now, class, what must we do before we ask the Lord to forgive us?" Quick as a flash a little boy replied, "Sin, teacher, we must sin." That's something with which none of us has any trouble at all.

The New Testament has five different words for this one word, "sin." One word in New Testament Greek says it means "missing the mark," not living up accurately to what God wants us to do and be. Another says sin is more like "stepping over the line," transgressing a boundary of behavior or attitude that

God has set before us. Another word means "slipping" as in a slippery, slidey place where we unintentionally fall. Another word means "lawless," that is, to do something which we know is breaking God's law. And, another still, means "failed duty." We fail to do what we could be doing.

As Karl Menninger, the noted psychiatrist reminded us in his book What Ever Happened to Sin, we no longer speak of Sin even in the church. We wish to be politically correct; we don't want a negative cultural bias to our language and, so, instead of talking about sinners we speak about persons of foibles. Instead of my Sin, we talk of my failures or my forgetfulness. Does that sound any better? Through our trickery of terminologies we sometimes strive to sheath our sophisticated semantics in a wide variety of fancy language. No wonder, however, as we watch our television screen from Oprah to Dr. Phil, we see people parading their peccadilloes and asking that we should understand and excuse them. We no longer think about people as doing right or wrong, but just how they have been subject to external circumstances, heredity or environment. Mrs. Bobbitt is regarded as someone who simply lost her mind one night, or, let's say the Menendez boys, after shooting their parents, reloading and shooting them again in the face and the chest, had been mistreated by their parents, were simply guilty of neglected childhood experiences. As far as Tonya Harding is concerned, she didn't live in a good neighborhood when she was a little girl - anything to excuse our errant behavior.

However, as the Bible reminds us: "All have sinned and fall short of the glory of God." There is in all of us a disposition to flaunt the will of God, to go our own way, and to miss the goal he has set for us. The Garden of Eden story, far from being a mythical account, is the dramatic representation of what you can read any day in the news headlines or in your own heart.

In offering this prayer, some say "trespasses" while other say "debts." This difference may raise unnecessary questions in a person's mind who wonders why all Christians cannot agree. While the difference cannot be justified, it can be explained. In the King James Version, the word in Matthew's account of the Lord's Prayer was translated as debts. Two verses later, Matthew uses another word, which means "trespasses." The word in Luke's account of the Lord's Prayer means sins. William Tyndale's earlier translation of the Bible rendered the first word in the Matthew account as "trespasses" and the Book of Common Prayer followed his example. Both words refer to the same problem, our sinning.

Unfortunately, for over 2,000 years Christians have not been able to get together in saying this prayer. How often have you felt awkward when you come to this part of the Lord's Prayer when you are in a public place? I have friends who say they simply don't say this part of the prayer. They just keep their lips shut so as not to be embarrassed with those who are trespassing all over the place. I know, when I'm in a public meeting place, I will say something about it so as not to cause people to choose up sides on this question. I was at an ecumenical gathering once where I made an announcement like this, and a Methodist speaker followed me. He said, "Bob Palmer is correct in using 'debts' rather than 'trespass.' You might expect a Presbyterian to know the better word since Presbyterians are sinning more than Methodists are in debt."

While either of the words is satisfactory, "debts" seem to some of us to the broader and more inclusive word. For it includes sins of omission—the good we fail to do—as well as the sins of commission—the wrong we do. Our whole life is one vast accumulative, unpayable debt to God. In fact, we are morally and spiritually bankrupt. Unless God, the Divine Creditor, forgives us, we are lost. Herein is the marvelous and loving grace of a redeeming God Who will step in the breach and do for us what we cannot do for ourselves. In fact he has already done so in His Son's atoning life and death. "God commended His love toward us in that while we were yet sinners Christ died for us."

When I attended the only Presbyterian Church in the United States in which we did not say "debts" but "trespasses," the Bryn Mawr Presbyterian Church in Philadelphia, I asked the minister why they said "trespasses" rather than "debts" He replied: "Very simply. Almost 200 years ago this church was founded by a group of bankers who refused to forgive 'debts', for any reason whatsoever." We are talking here about sinning. We are talking about Jesus' concern of our failure to live up to the best that he wants for us in our relationship with ourselves and with others and with him. It's sort of a boomerang petition: you forgive and you will receive forgiveness, not only with God, but with your neighbors as well.

In a church I once served, we substituted the word "sins" for both of the other possibilities, as they do in other places. While it seemed to solve this problem for our members, some visitors would occasionally comment that this word seemed unusual since they were accustomed to "debts" or "trespasses." Another solution is offered by the New English Bible which reads: "Forgive us the wrong we have done as we have forgiven those who have wronged us."

The main emphasis of this phrase in the Lord's Prayer, however, is not on sin, but on forgiveness. And Jesus is here saying that our personal relationships with one another and with the Lord God constitute a triangular circuit. When forgiveness creates a "short" anywhere in that circuit, it kills the whole circuit. So Jesus teaches us to pray, first, "Forgive us our debts."

On the surface this seems to be a simple and easy solution to sin, "Burn the candle at both ends and then blow the smoke in God's face." Why not? It's no skin off our teeth, for when the reckoning comes around, we sign the bill with a flourish— "Jesus Christ"—and assume that, like a soft indulgent father, God will settle the account. Now, of course, God's love is always open-ended, but in the divine economy forgiveness is a premium commodity. It hurts us to ask for forgiveness, however, to admit we are wrong. We blame someone else for our sin and that is paranoia: or we retreat into another personality, and that is schizophrenia.

The dear wife said to her husband, "Let me hear those three little words I long to hear?" He replied: "I love you." "Not those." "Which then?" "Just admit once that you were wrong, "I was wrong!" They're very hard for us to repeat. It hurts us to admit that we have done something wrong, so, we're tempted to blame somebody else.

It also hurts God to forgive. Jesus wrenched it out of death! If you are a Christian you are in the red, and the account is written in the blood of Jesus Christ!

We speak of this prayer as the Lord's Prayer. But it is not the Lord's Prayer in the sense that it was a prayer which the sinless Christ Himself offered. It is rather the prayer that He taught His disciples to pray. It is a prayer for sinners. A minister announced one Sunday that there were seven hundred and twenty-six sins. As a result, he was besieged with requests for the list, mostly from people who thought they were missing something. But most of us are well enough acquainted with sin to compile our own list.

By placing this petition in the Lord's Prayer, Jesus wants us to see sin not just as a list of moral violations, but as it affects our relationship with our Father in heaven. To see it this way makes sin grow even darker. For if the power behind the universe were sheer impersonal law, then our wrong thoughts and deeds would be sins against an all-powerful system of Law. But if the power behind the universe is a Father, then our wrong thoughts and deeds are sins against His love. And if it is bad to strike a blow at a fixed law, it is a thousand times worse to strike a blow at the heart of a Loving Heavenly Father. Indeed, to call God "Father" is ultimately to make sin intolerable. The greatest of all the parables, the story of the Prodigal Son, drives this lesson home. But not content with teaching it, Jesus Christ died to make it plain. For it was not law that men crucified on Calvary; it was God's holy love.

Crucified—but not killed. For at the Cross the father-heart of God passed the breaking point and refused to break. And if sin thus stands in a new light, so does God's victory over sin, which is forgiveness. "Can God forgive?" People asked that before Jesus came. The answer was more or less in doubt. But once you call God "Father" the question then becomes—how can God not forgive? Jesus daringly pictured God as not waiting for his shamed children to slink home, nor standing on his dignity when the children came, but reaching out to gather them, shamed and ragged as they were, back into His welcoming arms.

What happens in this "miracle" of forgiveness? Every one of us who can say, "I am a pardoned sinner," knows very well that this can never mean: "I do not sin any more."

There is really just one thing that forgiveness can do. Forgiveness does not take away the fact of sin. Nor does forgiveness take away the memory of sin. Nor does it take away all the consequences of sin. As Adam Bede the carpenter said, "Sin is like a bit of bad workmanship—you never see the end of the mischief it does. For there's a sort of damage that can't be made up for!"

But there is one thing that forgiveness does, that it always does. It reestablishes the old personal relationships that have been broken by sin and makes them deeper and sweeter, more meaningful. There is awakened love and responsive gratitude.

No parable can more than hint at the ways of God. But is not Jesus Christ a living thing, drawn from the life of the Father and stretched into our humanity so that new life flows into our lives and into our world? Thus every one can pray, "Forgive us our debts," and be assured of Divine forgiveness.

Second, Jesus teaches us to pray for forgiveness, "AS we forgive our debtors." This does not mean that God's forgiveness is limited by human conduct. This does not mean that our forgiveness automatically brings about God's forgiveness. Rather, it is a condition which is required. This means that because we have been forgiven by God, we are to forgive one another. Thus, when we pray, "Forgive us our debts, as we forgive our debtors," we are asking for that attitude of heart which will unite us with God.

Here is the really hard part of this petition. It is one thing to pray, "Forgive us our debts," but there's a condition here. It's like there's some kind of electric circuit and unless we forgive others, the electricity doesn't flow between us and God. So, we are to pray, "Forgive us as we forgive others." Why is it that we can accept God's forgiveness sometimes, but we have such a difficult time forgiving other people? We'd rather carry a grudge; we'd rather complain; we'd rather remember that slight, that wrong, real or imagined.

I love the story, coming out of the Appalachians Mountains, of a mountaineer sitting on his front porch, rocking his chair back and forth, and his hound dog lying beside him. The hound dog's tail was under the rocker, and the hound dog kept whining. Someone said, "Why is that dog whining, anyway?" The mountaineer said, "Well, you see, it's this way. It hurts him enough to whine but not enough to make him move." How many people do you know who would rather lie there whining about something that's happened, but they're not going to leave that place? It's more fun to whine than it is to move.

Let me tell you something that I've discovered in my own life. It's a beautiful truth: The only power I know to stop the stream of painful memories is to forgive what's been done. If you doubt this, just look at what's been happening in the Middle East for so long between Christian, Jew and Moslem. Paying back, paying back for 1500 years and the killing still hasn't stopped. Jesus says the only way we can really experience God's forgiveness and be at one is to forgive other people. It is as true with your neighbor down the block, as it is with foreign nations across the world. This does not mean that God's forgiveness is limited by us. It doesn't mean that God cannot forgive us if we have a hardened heart. Rather, it's a condition that He sets up because He made us, and He knows how we operate. When all else fails, read the directions. God's directions for life are, you can't do wrong and feel right; you can't receive forgiveness if you're unwilling to give forgiveness. So, when we pray, "Forgive us our debts as we forgive others," we are asking for that attitude of heart which will open us up to the future and leave the past behind.

A woman was bitten by a dog, and she was taken in the emergency room for an investigation as to whether she might have rabies. They took some of her blood and went to have it tested. While she was waiting there, sitting on the table, she was writing some things. One of the nurses said, "What are you writing?" She replied, "I'm making a list of people I intend to bite if I've got the rabies." Do you have a list of people you'd love to bite if you get the rabies? Do you have a pay back list? Are you carrying a grudge in your heart against anyone?

I remember when Harry Truman was president. He had a little motto on his desk which said, "The buck stops here." I made a little motto for my desk once, and it said "The hurt stops here." Until you can say that, you are never going to be rid of the past, never ever. Sir Walter Scott knew this. He had carried a grudge and he said, "You know, revenge is the sweetest morsel ever cooked in hell." I wonder if you've ever tasted that kind of morsel. Archie Bunker once said, "What's wrong with revenge? It's the perfect way to get even." But who are you getting even with, except hurting yourself?

Do you remember the story of the wife who said to her husband, "Alright, let's compromise: you admit your wrong and I'll accept your admission." That's the attitude we all have when it comes to settling an argument. You admit you're wrong, and then everything will be fine. The truth of the matter is that you cannot really pray this prayer at all unless you're willing to be the first to forgive. That's where the genius of the event comes in, be the first to say, "I was wrong."

The Apostle Paul has an exhortation which throws light on this petition: "Be ye kind one to another, tender-hearted, forgiving one another, even as God, for Christ's sake, hath forgiven you."

It is significant that the only petition of the Lord's Prayer which Jesus seemed to think needed further emphasis was this petition about forgiveness, for the record we have of the Lord's Prayer in Matthew's Gospel is followed by this comment: "If ye forgive men their trespasses, your heavenly Father will also forgive you; but if ye forgive not men their trespasses neither will your heavenly Father forgive your trespasses." In a similar passage, Jesus urges, "If thou art offering thy gift at the altar and there remember that thy brother hath aught against thee, leave there thy gift before the altar, and go thy way, first be reconciled to thy brother, and then come, and offer thy gift."

Do you remember the story Jesus told about the unmerciful servant who had a debt which must have seemed as great as our national debt. The man to whom he owed the money forgave him the debt. Then, after the Master's mercy was shown to him, the servant went straight from his knees to wring the neck of the poor fellow who owed him a very minor debt.

Jesus told this story to show that there is no forgiveness for people who are not forgiving: that all of God's forgiveness is wasted on us unless we are moved by His mercy to be merciful. There was nothing legal in his thought—if you do not forgive, God will not forgive. Rather, he was thinking of the corrosion in the human soul that harbors hate and resentment toward another, and how impossible it is for God's grace to live in a soul that is graceless.

The truth of the matter is that you cannot really pray this prayer unless you are willing to forgive. You are not saying to God, "Forgive me my debts." You are saying, "Forgive the man that I, myself, do not forgive." But the fact that you do not forgive him means that you do not desire him to be forgiven. Thus you are asking God for what you do not really desire at all.

Now and then, someone will say: "I can't forgive and forget." We are not required to forget, but to leave it in the past. We are not also required to reconcile and sometimes it is impossible anyway, since we can no longer have a relationship with another person. What we are required to do is forgive. As we recite in the Apostles' Creed: "I believe in the forgiveness of sins."

There is a story of King Albert of Belgium when, in the first World War, as the Germans ravished his little country, the Belgians were bitter and bowed down with sorrow. A small group of children with their teacher were gathered at a roadside shrine. They were saying the Lord's Prayer. Then they came to the words, "Forgive us our trespasses as we..." They stopped and could not go on. The teacher prodded, "But we must say it, "Forgive us our trespasses as we...." But then she too, stopped; and then another voice took up the words, "as we forgive those who trespass against us." It was the voice of King Albert as he stood behind their kneeling figures with bowed head and burdened heart. Remember that even on the Cross our King prayed, "Father forgive them, for they know not what they do."

Time and again in my ministry, and maybe in your life too, someone has come with a story about an abusive husband, about an unfaithful wife, about an uncaring parent, about a problem child, about a business relationship in which someone has cheated, but it always ends up with the same question: "Bob, how do you expect me to forgive that kind of behavior?" The only answer I can honestly give, because it is the only way I've ever been able to do it myself, is to say: "Because God empowers me to forgive the worst sins against me, when I remember how much I have been forgiven by my Lord Christ." Or as another friend of mine once said, "Until they do to you what they did to Jesus, you have no reason to complain." Without that empowerment I couldn't forgive anyone of anything.

"Amazing Grace, how sweet the sound
That saved a wretch like me,
I once was lost, but now am found,
Was blind, but now I see."
HYMN BY JOHN NEWTON

The only way to see clearly through the maze of forgiveness is to know that you have been forgiven.

General Oglethorpe, the founder of the colony of Georgia, said to John Wesley, "I will never be able to forgive that man." Wesley said: "Then you had better never commit a sin against that man." All have sinned and all may be forgiven. Simply put, I see this as a drama in four acts: we sin, we repent, we forgive, and we receive forgiveness. It all goes together.

The difficulty faced in forgiving someone has been movingly portrayed in Tennyson's, Idylls of the King. King Arthur has learned of his wife Guinevere's unfaithfulness. As she throws herself at his feet, Arthur did not say, "O that's all right dear, don't let it happen again," as if it didn't matter. Rather he says:

"Yet think not that I come to urge thy crimes;
I did not come to curse thee Guinevere,
I, whose, vast pity almost makes me die to see thee,
Laying there thy golden head,
My pride in happier summers at my feet.
Yet, all is past, the sin is sinned, and I.
Lo, I forgive thee as eternal God forgives."

Let me offer a perspective on forgiveness by the psychologist, Robert Enright who lists these nine steps involved in the process of Forgiveness: Don't deny feelings of hurt, anger, or shame. Rather, acknowledge these feelings and commit yourself to doing something about them.

- Don't just focus on the person who has harmed you, but identify the specific offensive behavior.
- Make a conscious decision not to seek revenge or nurse a grudge and decide instead to forgive. The conversion of the heart is a critical stage toward forgiveness.
- Formulate a rationale for forgiving. For example: "By forgiving I can experience inner healing and move on with my life."
- Think differently about the offender. Try to see things from the offender's perspective.
- Accept the pain you've experienced without passing it off to others, including the offender.
- Choose to extend goodwill and mercy toward the other; wish for the well-being of that person.
- Think about how it feels to be released from a burden or grudge. Be open to emotional relief. Seek meaning in the suffering you experienced.

- Realize the paradox of forgiveness: as you let go and
forgive the offender you are experiencing release and
healing.

Just before the end of World War II, C.S. Lewis spoke, on
the radio, about forgiveness, to fellow survivors and sufferers
in Great Britain. He told them, "Everyone says forgiveness is
a lovely idea, until they have something to forgive, as we have
in war time. And then to mention the subject at all is to be
greeted with howls of anger...Half of you already want to ask
me how I would feel if it was about forgiving, especially if you
were a Pole or a Jew? So do I. I wonder very much. I am not
trying to tell you what I could do. I could do precious little.
I am telling you what Christianity is. I didn't invent it. And
there, right in the middle of it, I am greeted by the words,
"Forgive us ... as we forgive..."

Though in our human companionship our own attitude
is never enough to guarantee the end of conflict and the
restoration of relationships, in our comradeship with God, our
attitude is the beginning. For God is always willing and ready
to be forgiving. "If we confess our sins, God is faithful and just
to forgive us our sins and to cleanse us of all unrighteousness."
That is the promise of our faith, the source of our hope, and
the process of our restoration. It is the continuation not of
the parable of the prodigal but of the parable of the sons and
daughters of the prodigal son. And as in the original, so in
the continuing story, a happy ending is guaranteed if we do
our part. If in coming to ourselves we accept the father's
acceptance of us even though we are unacceptable, he will
restore us to himself. He will give us back our sense of at-
one-ness with him, at right-ness with ourselves, at home-ness

in the universe and togetherness with others. So right will this feeling be that we shall know that we have made a good bargain, to have given up the bitterness and the barrenness of our unforgiven and unforgiving selves, in exchange for the restoration of right relationships with the Father of our spirits and the comrades of our human quest.

Look at your own heart. Have you become sullen, bitter, resentful, nursing a grudge against someone? If so—make things right now—and forgive. Is there some sin there that you are harboring? You cannot go on indefinitely shutting your eyes and ears to it. Perhaps this moment will be one of the finest hours of your life as you take this sin to God. I know there are many unadvertised needs existing beneath the respectable exteriors of our lives. And deepest among these needs—the unforgiven sins. Ask God to go with you, just now, into that secret place. Unlock that hidden door. Take out that unforgiven sin. For your soul's sake, for the sake of your loved ones, and especially for Christ's sake, get rid of it! And there is only one way to do it. Whatever theology you hold, it is the way of the Cross—penitence, confession, restitution, pardon. "Forgive us our debts, as we forgive our debtors."

Prayer: *Almighty and everlasting God, Who hates nothing that Thou hast made, and dost forgive the sins of all those who are penitent; create in us new and contrite hearts that we, worthily lamenting our sins and acknowledging our waywardness, may obtain of Thee, the God of all mercy, perfect remission and forgiveness; through Jesus Christ our Savior. Amen.*

8

 ## THE FATAL ATTRACTION

A little boy prayed, "Lord, if you can't make me a better boy, don't worry about it. I'm having a real good time as it is." Isn't this our spirit? Live it up! Live dangerously! By contrast, the one who prays, "Lead us not into temptation but deliver us from evil," sounds as if he is playing it safe, or trying to dodge the facts of life. But this is not the prayer of a weakling. It represents a healthy respect for the pitfalls of life, and a wholesome regard for the power of God to help us make our way through life. It is with these words that we conclude this prayer and go out to meet the world. We began this prayer with hallowing God's name and we conclude with facing life as it is.

What image comes to your mind when you hear the word "temptation"? Are you tempted to cheat? To lie? To be dishonest? To break a promise? There is a story which illustrates how our temptations change. A grandfather was walking with his grandson and they came upon a frog. The grandfather picked it up and was startled to hear the frog say: "Kiss me. I'm a princess and will do whatever you desire." The grandfather quietly picked up the frog and slipped him into his pocket. His grandson asked: "Why did you do that, she asked you to kiss her." Whereupon the grandfather replied, "At my age, I'd rather have a talking frog." At my age, my temptations are different then when I was twenty five years of age. I suspect that some of the saintliness oldsters are credited with has more to do with age than virtue.

Jesus Christ knows our plight in seeking to deal with temptations at any age. He Himself wrestled with temptation for forty days in the wilderness. He fully understands the tensions and turmoil that can be aroused in us because of temptation. When Jesus was coming out of his agony in the Garden of Gethsemane, he found Peter and James and John sleeping. He awakened them and said, "Watch and pray, lest ye enter into temptation." Here, in this sixth petition of the Lord's Prayer, Our Lord assures us of our heavenly Father's concern for us in our temptation and reminds us of his capacity to strengthen us in overcoming our temptation.

Let no one assume that God is a kind of divine seducer. James reminds us, "Let no one say when he is tempted that he is tempted of God." The New English Bible helps us here when it translates the verse: "Do not bring us to the test." While "temptation" may refer to those siren voices of flesh and spirit that would beguile us away from our spiritual concern, I believe it refers more to the very trial of our faithfulness to Christ. It is about the possibility that we shall turn our back on the kingdom.

The Greek word for temptation can mean "trial" or "test." It was this kind of testing that he experienced in the wilderness following his baptism. When he was in the wilderness for forty days, Satan tempted him in different ways from his devotion to the heavenly Father and his commitment to the kingdom here on earth. All these temptations – to turn stones into bread, to throw himself down from the temple and to be lifted up by angels—had one thing in common—they were all appeals to allow the self, and not God, to stand at the center of the universe.

There is nothing sinful about temptation. To be troubled by temptation may be a sign of spiritual health. Jesus Himself was tempted in all points such as we are, yet without sin. It is not temptation that ruins us, but yielding to the wrong temptation.

We are acquainted with the story of the little boy in New York City who prayed this clause of the Lord's Prayer: "Lead us not into Penn Station." We are also acquainted with the more serious problems of interpretation which we adults have with the phrase: *"Lead us not into temptation, but deliver us from evil."*

There is a difficulty in the word "lead," which some commentators feel should have been translated as "Have us not brought into temptation." The onus for seduction is thus laid on man or the devil rather than on God, the Deliverer. In the Greek, the verb is not "to lead" but "to allow." That puts the whole responsibility for sin where it belongs, upon the free, unfettered will of individual person. This prayer then says, in effect: "Dear Lord, keep us from gambling with our souls. Don't let us take a flier after every casual desire. Don't let us experiment with evil. Don't let us tinker with tragedy: Russian roulette with all the chambers loaded!"

There is an even greater difficulty in the word "temptation." If we take temptation as a lure toward evil, then the prayer seems to imply an unworthy view of God; for it is unthinkable that our heavenly Father would tempt us toward evil. And if we take temptation as meaning testing, then the prayer implies an unworthy attitude on the part of man; for we should not shrink from struggle. Some commentators have tried to ease this difficulty by pointing out that Jesus taught in Aramaic; a dialect of the Hebrew language. They then propose such a translation as: "Let us not succumb at the time of trial." Each of these interpretations sheds some light upon our Lord's meaning. And probably the prayer is best explained as a plea from a man who knows his own weakness. It is not an exercise in logic, but a cry of the soul.

In other times and places, some Christians have been tempted by persecution and great difficulties. Most Christians by contrast, have simply been too busy with other things; we have been careless about our faith; and we have encountered casual rather than transformable temptations. We need to hear our Lord's words in the gospel of Matthew: "Do not fear those who kill the body but cannot kill the soul, rather fear him who can destroy both soul and body in hell."

We are constantly faced by choices to make, to say something, to do something, to take something, or not, difficult choices, all the time. We call these choices temptations, or, in their more severe form, the fatal attraction. All of us have these temptations, Samson had his hair, Ted Williams had left field at Fenway Park, Bill Clinton had Big Macs and an extra order of French fries. For you, it could be a fine dinner and when you've finished with the entrée, a waitress comes with her dessert cart and says, "May I tempt you?" What is your fatal attraction?

Jesus said he knows our every temptation, but we like to "live it up," the "jet set," the "fast lane," "push the envelope," "brinksmanship." Jesus says, "Do not be led into temptation." We say, this sounds like the prayer of a wimp, to be afraid of

WHAT TO SAY WHEN WE PRAY:

temptation. Jesus says that it represents a healthy respect for life's dangers, for life's problems, for the evil that is everywhere present. "Live" spelled backwards is evil. It takes an expert to know this. We novices don't believe it. At a California beach, I asked a lifeguard, "Who is it who gets in trouble here?" He answered, "It's not a Californian; they know better. It's the person from North Dakota, who becomes burned from the sun, or gets caught in a rip tide, or pulled down in an undertow." Ask a bartender at a party, "Who gets in trouble here?" "Oh, it's not the one who's had a problem with alcohol and limits himself to two drinks. It's the one who boasts that he can handle his liquor. And the liquor handles him instead. So, we sometimes repeat, "Lead us not into temptation" in a careless way. It would help however, if we could ask ourselves what it means to be tempted. Some of us enjoy our temptations so much that our silent prayer is, "Don't bother not to lead us into temptation: we're rather liking it the way we are."

The words "lead us" actually mean "May we not be allowed to fall into temptation." That puts the responsibility where it belongs: on our own shoulders. The way our parents reared us it was our free will, and we could be succumbing to temptation or resisting it, or finding our own creative solution. Probably, the prayer is best explained as a plea for a person who is aware of her own weaknesses. It's not so much an exercise in logic as it is a cry of the soul to do the right thing. As such, what lessons may we learn from this petition in the Lord's Prayer? They say when E.F. Hutton speaks, everybody listens. When temptation speaks we all respond.

Therefore, when temptation speaks, we respond by saying Lead us not into temptation. This clause in the Lord's Prayer is linked with the clause before it by the conjunction "and."

"And, forgive us our debts, as we forgive our debtors. Lead us not into temptation." When a debt is forgiven there needs to be a follow-up to ensure a complete moral victory. So when you flee temptation, be sure you don't leave a forwarding address.

Forgiveness of sin is not as simple a transaction as running a cancellation line through an entry in the ledger, and thus settling the account. Hence when a sin is forgiven, the matter may be settled between the sinner and the one sinned against, but that is not all there is to it. For instance, you may tell a lie about someone, and that person may forgive it, saying, and "Let bygones be bygones." But if you think the matter is settled as easily as that, you may be tempted to presume on that person's repeated magnanimity and mercy. In families, we sometimes see children who come to presume on their parent's unfailing forgiveness. Likewise the temptation to presume on God's forgiving grace is very real. The thought, "Well, I got away with it again," may lurk in the mind of the forgiven sinner and make him prone to repeat the sin. Therefore, after we have prayed for forgiveness and received it, we should go on to pray that God lead us not into temptation.

Jesus said to the man whom he had healed after a sickness of thirty-eight years: "Sin no more, lest a worse thing come to thee." This bit of human wreckage had just been set upon his feet as a new man. But Jesus reminded him that it was sin that had forced him for more than half a lifetime to lie in impotent uselessness. Jesus warns further that for him to fall again will result in deeper tragedy than that from which he has just been delivered. And what he said to this man, and as he said to the woman caught in adultery, "Go, and Sin no more."

Temptation may follow in the train of forgiveness. The

penalty is gone, but the power of the sin may remain. Suppose you defraud someone and that person forgives you. The roots of greed may still remain in you. Too many of us seek to escape only the penalty of our sin and not really to purge ourselves from the sin itself. We need to go beyond forgiveness to find Him who "breaks the power of cancelled sin" and "sets the prisoner free" – free from the very taste for the sin itself.

Often we so halfheartedly come through our moral struggles with sin. We manage to resist the temptation and get through by the skin of our teeth, but we give the impression that we feel it might have been worth the loss of a tooth or two just to have had a taste of the forbidden fruit. The persons who go "all out" for sin play havoc with the world; but the world is not helped much by those who look "all in" trying to be good. No, goodness is commended to others by those who seem to enjoy it, by those spirits who carry their virtues with such grace that they make goodness attractive. Christ came to impart a radiant, abundant life—to make his followers, including us, more than conquerors in the fight with sin.

What we are saying here is that we are to be radiant exponents of the Way of Jesus Christ. He sets it before us, that we might attract others to follow, and not look for excuses that somebody else has forced us in our temptation to do wrong. Like that dear lady who loved to shop, and when she would come home, her credit card literally burning, and her husband burning, as well, she'd say: "I don't know why I did it; the Devil made me do it." He answered: "The next time you go shopping, and the Devil says that, just say 'Get thee behind me, Satan.' So, she came home the next evening with a gorgeous new dress, and her husband said: "I thought I told you to say 'Get thee behind me, Satan.' She replied: "I did, but Satan got behind me and said, 'That dress looks mighty cute from back here too.'" "We are surrounded on every side" say the saints, "by temptations of all kinds and descriptions."

Therefore, the true Christian prays not only for the forgiveness of sin but also for the strength to follow up with a clinching moral victory. Just as Hitler might have won the battle of Britain had he not failed to follow up his victory at Dunkirk, so many a battle with sin is lost through the failure to follow forgiveness with further moral effort against temptation.

In the second place, the petition "Lead us not into temptation" is a prayer for spiritual preparedness. It is linked to the clause which follows it as well as to the clause which precedes it: "Lead us not into temptation but deliver us from evil." Jesus was a master strategist in the campaign of life. Not only did he teach his disciples to clinch moral victories by follow-up, he also taught them to prepare for the moral fight ahead. Jesus is advising us not to borrow temptations. The road ahead has enough inevitable trials without running off into by-paths where we shall meet more. The pilgrim's progress is a stiff enough march at best without organizing voluntary track meets with temptation on the side just to see how much we can stand.

Like the line in My Fair Lady, when Professor Higgins musically protests the mispronunciation of the English, he compares them to the French: "The French never care what they do, actually, as long as they pronounce it properly." So it is with our sinning. While I have the highest respect for any man or woman who, in a time of danger, evidences heroism, on the other hand, I feel only pity for those who, in moral or physical issues, seem to tempt Providence by a false recklessness.

There is a curious difference between our estimates of the trouble we can stand and our estimates of the temptation we can withstand. Look ahead at a possible calamity and we say, "Oh, I could resist that," but we do not. When Jesus was foretelling how men would desert him in his hour of trial, Peter, with cocksure confidence, boasted, "Though all men shall be offended because of Thee, yet will I never be offended." But when his Lord was arrested, Peter's courage gave way and he denied him three times.

Jesus saw that if we are to be saved from evil we must establish our moral defenses far behind the line of external attack. "Ye have heard that it was said by them of old time, thou shalt not commit adultery; but I say unto you, that whosoever looks on a woman to lust after her hath committed adultery with her already in his heart And if thy right eye offend thee, pluck it out." Such was the Master's sharp, surgical way of saying that our moral bastions must be built at the eye gate and the ear gate, where temptations begin their deadly work of undermining our moral defenses. If we are to be delivered from tomorrow's sins, we must be led away from the temptation to bitter brooding over past wrongs and to secret hoping for future revenge.

Do you remember that we used to talk about the distant early warning in our International defense systems? That system of defenses in outer Alaska would warn us of any incoming missile from the North? We do not need to wait until we actually do something, or until the moment of temptation. Remember the distant early warning of your eyes, your fantasies. When I was a child and I heard this saying of Jesus, "The one who lusts after someone else is guilty of adultery," I never could understand that. What it means for me now, I believe, is that you should watch out what your fantasies are, what do you dream of doing, what do you think you'd like to be, how do you see yourself behaving? What gets through the eye gate will get to the heart, and what gets to the heart will become an action. That's what Jesus is talking about here. "The 'me' I see is the me I'll be."

Third, this last petition of the prayer, "Deliver us from evil," is so closely connected with the previous one, that it, not is may seem merely to repeat it. This is perhaps the reason why it does not appear in the Gospel of Saint Luke. Yet it is a new and separate petition which is necessary to complete the other.

I'm reminded here of a novel, later made into a motion picture, by James Dickey called Deliverance. It's a mythological picture of what we're talking about. It concerns four men from a city who embark on a canoe trip down a wild white-water river in north Georgia. On the way, they are attacked by some murderous locals. After a hair-raising escape they complete their trip down the river canyon, with one of the locals stalking and shooting at them from above. By the end of the story they are barely delivered, but their minds are scarred. Dickey says life is like a passage down a dangerous way where the devil is waiting to devour us.

So we see that this petition is not anti-climactic. Acknowledging all that the prayer previously mentions, now we pray that we will hold on to our faith, with God's help, and never lose it. As it were, we are in life's canyon, and the devil has us in his sights. But we can count on our deliverance, for we know who can deliver us.

When we pray, "Deliver us from evil," we may be speaking of evil in the abstract, or evil in general, but more probably, the petition refers to the "evil one" – the devil himself. Most people do not believe in the devil today, and therefore do not feel it necessary to ask to be delivered from him. To this thought let me say that our attitude toward evil is not what it was a generation ago. Then, many considered evil to be an imperfection, something that was in the process of being outgrown and sloughed off. Today evil has been incarnated in human beings to a degree that we should never have thought possible.

From the use that Christ made elsewhere of the word here translated "evil," it seems clear that in this prayer Christ is telling us to pray that we may be kept out of the power of the devil, and that we may be delivered from his influence.

One of the most beautiful paraphrases of the Lord's Prayer ever written is found in Dante's Purgatory where the sixth petition is rendered as follows:

"Our virtue which so soon doth harm receive,
Put not to peril with our ancient Foe;
But from his evil sting deliverance give."

The Apostle Paul also said that in our warfare we wrestle not with the flesh and blood merely, but with the mysterious and powerful source of evil, against principalities and powers. "Therefore," he says, "put on the whole armor of God, that ye may be able to withstand the evil one."

Recently in speaking with some college students I was asked: "Since you are a minister, you probably don't know; but anyhow, why shouldn't we be promiscuous and enjoy ourselves, since everybody else is?" I answered that we clergymen are not as isolated as he thinks. We do see sin. We see it at the sleazy end of its innocuous beginning, when the mask is off, and the sinner sits down and sobs at what has been committed. We see it when it is too late. Few people recognize it when it first arrives. Nobody ever says to me: "Say, Reverend, I am thinking more or less of going out and committing adultery; all right with you?" No one says that. But, when he has been discovered, when the moral ambulance comes screaming for the soul, and when all Hell breaks loose, then everybody sees it at the end. Yes, sin is a dangerous foe, and a deadly enemy. God doesn't lead us into it, but only He can help us out of it.

A strange thing about sin is that the more we practice it, the less we know about it. Practice make imperfect. C.S. Lewis, with his surgical precision, cuts us to the core at this point: "When a man is getting better, then he understands more clearly the evil that is in him. When a man is getting worse, he understands his own badness less and less. A thoroughly bad man thinks that he is all right!"

It is the nature of evil to disguise itself. It does not come announced. When did you last see sin in Technicolor, advertising in advance, and pasted up with placard to identify it? No, most sin is average and normal. At its most insidious, it seems most innocent, and it is far more likely to be found behind the veil than underneath the rouge.

On the other hand, the more you avoid evil, the better you can meet it. No, I am not advocating the nunnery and the hermitage. Sin does exist. Christ on the cross was not a Kodachrome projected on a cloud bank. But, avoid it while you can. Oscar Wilde's name has been synonymous with human frailty. He simply could not overcome his desires and he advised, "The only way to be rid of temptation is to yield to it." So, one conquers by compliance. These are the famous last words of the lost souls of the world.

I suppose some of us have our price as to when we will yield to temptation. George Bernard Shaw, another writer, met a lovely, young woman at a party, and he asked: "Would you spend the night with me for a million pounds?" She replied, "Yes". "Would you spend the night with me for half a million pounds?" "Yes." "Would you spend the night with me for ten pounds?" She said, "What do you think I am?" He answered, "We have already established what you are, and we're just now haggling over price." Does every one have a price? What would it take to have you sell out to temptation?

Over against this kind of thinking we have the triumphant truth of God, as stated in the Bible where Jude writes: "Now unto Him that is able to keep you from falling, and to present you faultless before the presence of His glory with exceeding joy." In other words, we begin to realize that we are made for victory instead of defeat, that we are to overcome evil rather than to be overcome by it. Triumphantly we may declare with the Apostle Paul: "I can do all things through Christ who strengthens me."

We have seen that while God tempts no man, He clearly permits trials, troubles and testing to come to every one of us. When they come, then we pray to God, "Deliver us from evil." Temptation is but a fork in the road with an upper and lower road. God is always present at the scene, inviting us to take the upper road. He is always there to undergird us with the "everlasting arms." He can "deliver us from evil." That is the affirmation of this prayer. Temptation to evil, then, is also temptation to good, if we only realize it. Every moral crisis is double; it really offers two choices, not one.

A person who is never tempted is morally anemic. He may not do any harm in life, but the trouble is he will not do much good either. Are you tempted to lust? Then remember you are being tempted at that very moment to choose the highest type of love. Are you tempted to be dishonest? You are also being tempted to find integrity of character. Are you tempted to anger? You are also being tempted to self-control. Are you tempted to doubt God? You are also being tempted to a deeper faith. You see, there are two paths out of every temptation experience—the alluring path of evil, but the equally alluring path of good.

Dwight L. Moody, the evangelist took the money he received in his campaigns, and built the Northfield Schools. There, on a certain hill, he once wanted to build a chapel. With his typical humor, he called that place "Temptation Hill." Moody explained, "Someday, someone just won't be able to resist the temptation of building a church there." And this minute, high on "Temptation Hill," stands one of New England's loveliest chapels.

Do not forget God's alternative, the temptation to good in every temptation of evil. So enter your spiritual and moral battles with joy, unafraid, for on every Temptation Hill of your life Jesus Christ can enable you to live your life to the glory of God.

I have learned two lasting lessons from this phrase, "Lead us not into temptation." We follow this petition because Christ captures our imaginations. Christ enables us, by his Spirit, to paint on the walls of our imagination portraits of the persons we can be. "As a man thinks in his heart, so is he." Aren't we all tempted by pictures of what we would like to be? Picture yourself as a child of God living up to the best that you can be. Paint a picture for yourself. That's what advertising is doing for you every minute of every day.

We are continually accosted by advertisements—picture yourself driving this car, picture yourself wearing that dress, picture yourself taking that trip, picture yourself doing this. Christ says that we should picture ourselves being meek, then becoming the loving and the peacemakers.

The second thing I've learned from this petition is not only for us to paint these pictures on the imagination of our minds, but to travel with creative companions, companions who will sustain us and bless us by their example and by their teaching. Isn't that one of the reasons we come to church, for the companionship, the comradeship of fellow Christians? Jesus was ready to face the impersonal mob on Maundy Thursday, but, when things became difficult, he called The Twelve to be alone with him, intimately, at the supper on Thursday. When one betrayed him, he took the eleven into a garden to be alone with them. Before he was arrested he took three to Gethsemane to pray, and finally, he was all alone. Let me tell you this, dear friends, we will walk alone when we must, but let us stand together when we can. Here is the secret of resisting temptation: We must not trifle with trouble by looking for it, for we can triumph over trouble when it looks for us. "Lead us not into temptation, deliver us from evil." As the poet puts it, and we all sing the hymn:

> *"Have we trials and temptations,*
> *Is there trouble anywhere?*
> *Precious Savior, be our refuge.*
> *Take it to the Lord in prayer."*

Prayer: *O God, keep us this day and night from deliberately or carelessly allowing temptation's appeal to continue until we finally yield. This we ask in the power of Jesus, Who, though tempted in all points even as we, was yet without sin. Amen.*

9

WHO IS IN CHARGE HERE?

I hope that everyday this week and in all the weeks to come we may all be in prayer for our nation, for peace, for termination of conflict, for our President and for those in positions of authority, for those serving in the Armed Forces, the Intelligence community, for those at home who have seen loved ones go away, or have even lost loved ones, for those who feel the hurt and harm of war firsthand, for justice and for mercy. As we seek an answer to the question, "Who's In Charge Here?"

This has been a question raised by God's people throughout the centuries. And I have heard it raised by many to whom I have ministered, especially when things are going not the way we would like. So there are two passages which I would like to share, one from the Old and one from the New Testament, to illustrate the final phrase which we are looking at today, in the closing words of The Lord's Prayer; "Thine is the Kingdom, the Power and the Glory forever."

Those of you who have looked in your Bible Reference notes will note that in the first century, this phrase was in the margin of the manuscript. It was not until the second century, at least, that it found its way into the body of the Lord's Prayer.

I was trying to explain this to a fundamentalist friend of mine who strictly followed a literal interpretation of the scriptures. And he responded by saying: "Well, if Jesus didn't say this, he certainly should have said it."

The point is that it was common in Hebrew prayers to respond to what had been said by ascribing to God Kingdom, Power and Glory, and that we do in this phrase. The first passage is from Chronicles where we see David on his death bed. David, the Great King of Israel, no longer able to rise and grapple with lions or fight Giants, but knowing never the less who was in charge of the Kingdom which he had led. We read that David praised the Lord in the presence of the whole assembly, saying: "Praise be to you, O Lord, God our Father Israel from everlasting to everlasting. Yours, O Lord, is the greatness and the power and the glory and the majesty and the splendor for everything in heaven and earth is yours. Yours, O Lord, is the kingdom. You are exalted as head over all. Wealth and honor come from you. You are the ruler of all things. In your hands are strength and power to exalt and give strength to all. Now our God, we give you thanks and praise in your glorious name." So spoke David, the great king of Israel.

And when David's descendent, our Lord himself, was born in David's city, he became King of the Jews in another sense. This is what he had to say about the kingdom and what it is like. "Jesus asked, 'What is the Kingdom of God like?' What shall I compare it to? It is like a mustard seed, which a man took and planted in his garden. It grew and it became a tree and the birds of the air were perched in its branches.'" And again he asked, "What shall I compare the Kingdom of God to? It is like yeast that a woman took and mixed into a large amount of flour until it worked all through the dough."

Who's in charge here is a question perhaps all of us ask all the time. What a time we are living through. We need to be in prayer for our world that we are viewing and experiencing. It seems that almost constantly we have to face some kind of conflict, whether we want to or not.

And many of us ask the question at a time like this, or when we are undergoing personal setbacks, "Who's in charge here?" We, of the Christian faith, can answer "God is on the throne." Particularly as Presbyterians we emphasize the sovereignty of God recognizing that there are such things as the breaks and chance. Overall, God is in charge of the world. His providence governs the affairs of nations as well as persons. I know sometimes in my own life when I have been facing some difficulty, I have reminded myself, "God is on the throne."

Since that is the case, we can affirm that God is in charge, that we are part of a larger picture, that we are not all alone on the fringe of history. We are part of the Kingdom, part of God's purpose which he has for each of us. I saw an interesting illustration of this from a friend of mine, Tony Compolo, who teaches at the Eastern College in Pennsylvania. He told some of us the story of driving down the turnpike in Philadelphia in his old green Chevy when he had a blowout. He pulled over, got out, left his radio on, took the tools and the fresh tire out and was kneeling on the pavement changing the tire, when over his radio, he heard this announcement, "There is some guy by a green Chevy kneeling on the pavement, clogging traffic, which is now backed up for three miles." There was a helicopter overhead announcing this. Tony said, "You know, even though it was only fixing a flat tire, it was nice to be a part of a larger picture."

Thine is the kingdom, the power and the glory. We are

not all alone in this world. We are set against the background of eternity and the will of God. Let's take each word and see what fresh meaning we may derive from looking at it carefully. Thine is the first word. It all belongs to God and we are a part of his kingdom, power and glory, forever. Notice that in the Lord's Prayer, the Kingdom is spoken of, not once, but twice. The first time we pray Thy Kingdom come. Here at the end we say Thine is the kingdom. It is like that grand anthem from the Halleluiah Chorus, pianissimo, The kingdom of this world IS BECOME THE KINGDOM OF OUR LORD, JESUS CHRIST. And that is what this phrase declares.

We, in America, have trouble with kings and kingdoms. We are a democracy, a republic. When we see kingdoms today like the United Kingdom, a King (Or Queen) seems almost peripheral to the course of history. But, when this word was used in the New Testament it signified power. When we talk about the kingdom of God, we mean the rule of God, the will of God, the way of God, the work of God in our world and we want to be associated with it, hooked up to God's purpose for the world. And that is what we declare when we say "Thine is the kingdom." Can you not just imagine David? David who would grapple with a lion, and flog giants had all the charisma of a John Kennedy, the military prowess of a Dwight Eisenhower, the physical strength of a Michael Jordan, and the poetic sense of a Robert Frost. Who ruled Israel for 40 years! Made it a great nation. Established a capital in Jerusalem. Decided what the temple would be like. On his death bed, saying before all his advisers and generals, Thine is the Kingdom, the Power and the Glory. And we see this echoed in the words of Jesus.

When we say these words today I suspect there are some who when they pray, in the back of their minds are asking,

"Is this really that kind of a world? Is God really in charge?" I enjoyed reading a book some time ago called Life with Father. In this book the author says, "My Dad thought he was a Christian, acted and spoke and prayed like he was living in a poorly managed guest house, and there was a constant complaint about the food and the heating and everything connected with that guest house." I suspect that is the way some of us pray. Dear Lord, why did this happen to me? Why did that happen to her? Everything can be going our way except one little area and that little area can become so large that we magnify it in our own thinking and we complain to God because one thing is not quite the way we think it should be. We wonder if God is really calling the shots.

There is a story about a high school football team. It was the final quarter with three minutes to go. The home team was on the 30 yard line and the score was 32 to 31 - they were ahead. It had been a difficult fight however, and the first string and second string quarterbacks had been injured. So the coach had no other alternative but to send in the Freshman Third String quarterback who had never played in a game. The coach told the young man that they did not have any time-outs left and that he should remember these four plays, because I cannot call them again. I do not want any improvisation on your part. Remember, I am the coach and I call the plays and don't drop the ball. These are the four plays. First of all, send the left halfback around one end and ask him to take as much time as possible, just killing the clock. Next, give it to the right halfback and tell him to do the same thing. For the third play, even though this might be difficult for you, I want you to hold onto the ball and try a quarterback sneak through the line. Most important of all, on the fourth down have the punter kick that ball as far as he can. No improvisation. So, the quarterback did as he was told.

The first halfback didn't make it more than a yard or so. The right halfback did not do any better. And then it was the quarterback's turn. He tucked the ball in and he started running and, lo and behold, the center cleared a hole in the line and the quarterback ran all the way down the field to the one foot line. What did he call for? He punted. Just like he was told. It went out of the park.

Well, they brought the ball up to the 20 yard line, and the clock ran out and the home team won 32 to 31. But during the celebration of the victory afterward, the Coach said, "Come here young man, will you? I want to ask you a question. What in the world was going through your mind when you punted the ball?" Well, Coach, I was thinking 'I have the dumbest Coach anyone ever had.'"

Anybody here ever felt that way, that God was calling the wrong play? Surely there must be a better way of running this world than that. Surely, indeed. But Thine, O Lord, is the Kingdom and we are to thank God for the Kingdom. It is his. That is what Paul declares when he says, "We know that in all things God works to bring about good for those who love him, for those who are being called according to his purpose." And then you turn a few pages over into the book of Revelation and you hear, "Worthy is the lamb who is slain from the foundation of the world, and to him be all the glory and honor, dominion and power forever more."

Those New Testament writers, in spite of the terror and the conflict and the warfare of their day knew that things were in God's hands. Thine is the Kingdom and Thine is the power. God has the power of life. He gave life to this universe with all the myriad of stars, the sun the moon, the heavens and the Earth. He gives life to you, to me.

What I wonder about sometimes is why some people so concerned about the mystery of death insist on missing the miracle of life, which to me is just as difficult to understand. Clearly the miracle of life on this Earth is the power of God in our world.

We talk about power and are very much impressed with power in America. We hear that Einstein is quoted as saying there is enough power in a glass of water to drive a ship across the oceans. Or we read of a Donald Trump who can build skyscrapers in New York City and buy blocks of land in Manhattan. Create office buildings and towers. Go down to Atlantic City and see huge hotels and casinos and open multi-story multi tiered hotels in Miami and Chicago. We say, "That's financial power."

During the Nixon Administration, Henry Kissinger was known as a power broker. We read how he was jetting about from one country to another, particularly in the Middle East showing America's power to bring peace in the world. Some of you may remember Henry Kissinger and how he sounded and what he looked like. He would often be in a social setting and he would be surrounded inevitably by tall gorgeous women. He married a statuesque model. A friend of Henry's said, "Henry, how in the world does a fat, little character like you, get all these beautiful women?" And he replied, "Power is the ultimate aphrodisiac." And I guess there is something to be said about the aphrodisiac of power in our society. Jesus has a different kind of power; God has a different kind of power in this life. The power of his life and love. And that is what he is showing in this parable that he tells us about the kingdom of

God. He doesn't compare it to a vast army. He says, "What's the kingdom of God like? Well, it's like a tiny mustard seed."

Did you ever see a mustard seed? I know when I was a child in Sunday school I got a little marble and in the middle of it was a dot, and that was a mustard seed. They used to have them on necklaces that the girls would wear. Mustard seeds. That is what the kingdom is like. I was told that a hawk, sitting on top of the Empire State Building has such vision that he can spot a dime on the sidewalk. Jesus is telling us that we have to have kingdom eyes to perceive the kingdom. We have to be alert and alive to the potentialities of the kingdom that sometimes are as small as a mustard seed, but can grow as tall as a tree.

When I served a large church in Lincoln, Nebraska I remember we bought and bulldozed an entire city block and we poured concrete over the whole thing in a tiered parking lot. Oh, we were so pleased. And week in and week out these trucks would come and pour the concrete, smooth it out. It was a very fine looking structure, destined to last a long time. The next spring, as I walked out into that parking lot, in several spots, do you know what I saw? Little daisies sprouting up though the cracks in that concrete. Talk about power, that was power.

When our recent granddaughter was born, I had access to some book that had a page, and on that page was a little bitty spot, no bigger than a pin point. And it said, "This is the size of the egg where the baby started." And that contains all the eggs that mother will ever have. That contains the slant of her nose, the color of her eyes, the texture of her hair, the look of her complexion, her capacity for growth and personality. All that in something the size of a mustard seed. We need kingdom eyes to realize that God is at work in our world.

I read a book sometime ago, written by John Savage. It has in it a narrative between a father and his junior high daughter. She is complaining, "Nobody loves me, Daddy. The kids in school don't treat me with respect. The teachers don't notice me, nobody loves me." So, the father sits her down and says, "Does your mother get up every morning and make you breakfast?" "Yeah." "Your mother is saying 'I love you.'" "Did I tell you yesterday to fasten your seat belt when we got in the car?" "Yeah." "I was saying, 'I love you.'" "Did someone tell you last week that she liked the way your hair was done?" "Yeah". "She was saying, 'I love you.'" "Didn't your dentist tell you last month that he was going to correct your malocclusion?" "Yeah." "Well, your dentist was saying, 'I love you.'"

The little girl said, "Gee, I never knew my dentist loved me before." Love can be shown in such subtle ways if we have ears to hear and kingdom eyes to see the way in which God is working in our world. There is no question about it friends, this is the way God is working within us and around us.

I saw a wonderful illustration of this in something that Mikhail Gorbachev said after he visited this country on one occasion. He told of the funeral of Leonid Brezhnev, the great President of the Soviet Union when it was at its power apex. His body was laid out in a coffin in the Kremlin. A number of dignitaries spoke and after awhile they filed by the casket. And just before two soldiers were to close the casket and have it carried out to Red Square, they deferred to Brezhnev's wife and she walked over and she looked in the casket, and she made the sign of the cross. And then she leaned down over her husband and she made the sign of the cross over Brezhnev's body and then kissed him. Gorbachev said that made such an impression on him. And "I remembered that my own mother had me baptized when I was a child. What a courageous expression of spiritual power."

God is at work in our world in ways beyond our understanding, if we just had the eyes and the faith to see. Thine is the kingdom and the power and the glory. Perhaps you watch the annual Academy Awards. They have been going on now for 80 years. Did you know that Oscar, Mickey Mouse and I all have the same birthday? What a claim to fame. Mary Lou and I had the opportunity to visit one of these ceremonies one year and of course we have seen it on television many times. As a matter of fact, except for the Super Bowl, more people will see the Oscar presentations than any other television program ever broadcast. You've seen these gigantic statues and the stars with the glittering lights and the red carpet and all the pageantry and all the glory of who the winners are going to be. And yet, I saw a survey this week in which Americans were asked the question, "What was the best picture last year?" "Who won the best actor and the best actress award?" Only ten percent of Americans could remember one year later who had won the Oscar. The glory fades so quickly doesn't it? But Thine is the glory for God and we give God the glory forever.

Thomas Grey said once, "The paths of glory all lead to the grave." We become so obsessed with our own glory. There is a story coming out of the first Gulf War of a Major who was suddenly promoted to a Bird Colonel and he was very impressed with himself. He was sitting in his office looking at his desk and the telephones he had there and the carpet on the floor and the eagle on the door and a Private knocked on the door and came in. This was the first visitor the Colonel had and he wanted to impress this poor Private. So he picked up the phone and he said, "Yes, General Schwartzkopf. No, Norm, I wouldn't do it that way at all, what I would do is first, I would send in the cruise missiles and then I'd have the carrier planes hit Baghdad and after that I would send in the heavy armor and the tanks and only then would I send in the infantry. I knew you would agree with me General, thank you."

"Now, private, what is it you want?" "Well, I was just coming to connect your telephone, Sir," Wouldn't you have loved to have been that Private??

The glory that fades all too quickly. And that is why we say that to God the Kingdom, the power and the glory, belongs.

During the Napoleonic campaigns, one of the British Admirals was feeling very proud. He had just achieved a victory and was sailing back to England. The fog rose, as it often does, off the coast of England, so he had all the running lights turned on. Lo and behold, he saw some lights coming toward him and he called out over the megaphone, "Ahoy, there. Turn to your Starboard or we will run you over. This is Her Majesty's Man of War Battle Ship." And he heard back from the light, "Ahoy, there, turn to your port or you'll hit her Majesty's light house."

There are some things that remain and some things that change. Jesus gave us a prayer in which we say "forever". It's not just the glory, but there is a comma after glory, so we say, the kingdom and the power and the glory, forever. When we were kids we used to drive along country roads in our old Chevy and we'd see painted, maybe on a rock or some kind of a bulletin board along side of the road, a sign like, "Prepare to meet thy God." We would joke about it at the time, but it was pointing us to the fact that we are created for something more than this day. We are created for a life beyond with God.

Sometime ago, when the Presbyterian Church had more money, it sponsored a series of radio advertisements that were written by Stan Freburg. I remember one of them. There were a couple of golfers who were coming off the 18th hole and the one said to the other, "Let's get together sometime and we can talk business. Here is my card." And he handed his business card to the other golfer. The other golfer picked up the business card and said, "I see that you are working for the First National Bank. The Vice President. I notice also that the name and the title are penciled in." The fellow says, "Yeah, we are all penciled in, aren't we?"

I'm penciled in. But we have children who are penciled in before they grow up. We have young married couples who are penciled in before they mature. We have babies penciled in before they become adults. We have marriages penciled in before we ever know the ending.

I saw a statistic that said 50% of all marriages end in divorce. Do you know where the other 50% end? In death! We are all bound for the same place. We are bound for glory through faith in Jesus Christ. We believe that.

When I was serving a church in Oklahoma City, I had a funeral one day and by the time I got to the cemetery outside of the city, the monument had already been laid in the ground. The deceased was kind of a cowboy preacher type of a man and the monument read, "He taught mortal men about immortality." That is what we come here for, isn't it, to be reminded that we are not merely strangers on the passing scene that will soon be forgotten. We are bound for glory with our eternal Father.

Heywood Broun was a fine writer, but he was also a

cynic. About middle age, however, he became converted to the Christian faith and he started writing Christian articles instead. When he died, Christopher Morley spoke at his funeral. Christopher Morley said, "Heywood Braun was a man who liked to be thought of as a man about town. But the longer he lived; the town he was most concerned about was the City of God." John Baillie, one of my theology teachers at Edinburgh said, "When a person becomes a Christian and knows God through Jesus Christ, already a great transformation has begun and it will continue when that person dies and goes to heaven."

There is within you now the Kingdom, the power and the glory, forever. When I was at Princeton I had a speech professor named Bill Beeners. He had certain pet peeves. One of them was when people said the Lord's Prayer and they petered out at the end. He said, "The way most of your preachers pray, it winds down: 'Thine is the kingdom, the power, the glory, forever, Amen'." As if you are running out of steam. What you ought to say is, Thine is the Kingdom, the power and the Glory, Forever, AMEN!

Prayer: *O God our Father, remind us that this world does not have the final word; that word belongs to you, and your kingdom, power and glory, forever. Amen.*

10

THE AMEN CORNER

Mary said to Martha, "I wish my preacher was more like yours. When your preacher says, 'In conclusion,' he concludes. When my preacher says, 'Lastly,' he lasts."

Is this the significance of "Amen," a kind of "Roger and Out" to conclude the prayer? No, it is much more. It's the personal exclamation point at the end of the prayer to our Father in heaven.

Its significance can be found in Paul's writings where the word Amen is used. Paul normally did not equivocate. But in this instance his word was being challenged and his integrity was being questioned. Integrity is a priceless commodity. George Burns once said, "To be successful in life, you must have integrity when you speak. Once you learn to fake that, you have it made."

It seems that Paul had intended to go to Macedonia. On his way, he hoped to stop in his beloved Corinth. On his way back, he also planned to return to Corinth. But his plans were changed. As a result some people in the Corinthian Church were attributing to him the wrong motives. They said that he had waffled, that he spoke out of one corner of his mouth one day and the other corner another day. Paul uses the word

"Amen" to affirm that he means what he says. When he writes a letter, it is to be believed. Since this modern translation by Eugene Peterson called The Message strikes closer to Paul's spirit. There the words for Amen are translated, "Confident of your welcome, I had originally planned two great visits with you. Coming by on my way to Macedonia province, and then again on my return trip. Then we could have had a bon voyage party as you sent me off to Judea. That was the plan. Are you now going to accuse me of being flippant with my promises because it didn't work out? Do you think I talk out of both sides of my mouth? A glib 'Yes' at one moment, a glib 'No' the next? Well, you are wrong. I try to be as true to my word as God is to his. Our word to you was not a careless 'Yes' which was cancelled out by an indifferent 'No'. How could it be? When Silas, Timothy and I proclaimed the Son of God among you, did you pick up on any Yes and No, off and on again waffling? Was it not a clean, strong, 'Yes'? Whatever God has promised gets stamped with the 'Yes' of Jesus. In him, this is what we preach and pray, the great Amen. God's 'Yes'. And our 'Yes' together gloriously evident. God affirmed us making us a sure thing in Christ. Putting his 'Yes' within us. By his spirit he has stamped us with his eternal pledge. A sure beginning of what he is destined to complete."

This marked a genuine difference between the Christian and Jewish use of the word "Amen." The Jews pronounced the word as a liturgical response, as a word of personal ratification, as an exclamation of praise. But the Christians went farther and said it with the sense that it was more powerful than any word spoken in their own names.

In fact, the early Christians went even farther than this, and identified Christ himself as the Amen, as the one causing the prayer to come true. When John was inspired to write the book of Revelation, he saw the risen Lord in a vision. Jesus told him to write letters to each of the seven churches of Asia Minor. When he came to the seventh, the church of Laodicea, Jesus commanded him to write: "The words of the Amen, the faithful and the true witness, the beginning of God's creation" (Revelation 3:14). Jesus himself was speaking as the Amen, the one making God's kingdom to come on earth!

My home church in Chicago is the Fourth Presbyterian Congregation on North Michigan Avenue. Some of you may have seen it, across from the Hancock Center. It was designed by Ralph Adams Cram and is a huge Gothic-like structure fashioned after Chartes Cathedral in France. It has soaring arches, flying buttresses, magnificent stained glass, padded walnut pews, and figures on top of the columns representing the various writers of the New Testament. It so happened one Sunday that a visitor, a Baptist woman, had slipped into the front pew to worship. As the preacher from his elevated pulpit began to speak, she shouted, "Amen, Brother." He tried to ignore it and went on.

He made another point and she said, "Praise the Lord, Preacher. Amen." With that, the head usher came down the aisle, leaned over to her and whispered, "Madam, I will have to ask you to be quiet."

She said, "But I was just praising the Lord."

"Madam, this is no place to praise the Lord like that."

Have you ever felt that way in a Presbyterian church? We Presbyterians talk about order and ardor. In most congregations at the top of the worship service, it says, Order of Worship. I tried to change that emphasis in one of the Churches we served, and I wrote Ardor of Worship. Time and again people would stop me and say, "Bob, don't you know how to spell order?" So, I simply wrote, Celebration of Worship and let it go at that.

Amen is a mighty word. If it were just to conclude a prayer, I would not comment on the subject. But it is far more than that. In fact, it has many meanings in the Old and in the New Testaments. It is just a little four letter word, and yet, as you know, many four letter words mean a lot and can get us in trouble sometimes.

In Presbyterian churches, we often say Ah-men. In less liturgical services, we hear A-men. I was told in Princeton Seminary that when you say it, it is pronounced A-men, when you sing it, it is Ah-men. We do not intend to be politically correct by changing it to Ah-women instead of Ah-men. Ah-men is what Liz Taylor says when she walks into a room.

In the Hebrew language, the word means "So be it" or "Thus let it be." In its first usage, it signified a solemn participation in the placing of a curse on someone who had violated sacred law. It was the people's part in a ritualistic action, and expressed their corporate unity in the action being taken. As such, the word "Amen" has remained the peoples' assent to worship or corporate action. And, in Christendom's less formal liturgies, it is often freely used to express the people's agreement to what is said. As the Westminster Shorter Catechism puts it: "In testimony of our desire and assurance to be heard, we say 'Amen'". This is the final peal of the trumpets!

"Amen" is a Hebrew word, the literal meaning of which is strength, and the derived meaning is "certainty." "Amen" was used in ancient Israel as an oath. When a man was stating something with the utmost conviction, he would begin a declarative statement with the word "Amen"—of a certainty—

of a truth—let it be so. This is not the expression of a pious hope, but a deeply felt conviction. As you know, the ancient Jews never employed the name of God in an oath. But there is a peculiar passage in the prophet Isaiah which speaks of "The God of amen." So that the force of "amen" in ancient Israel was, in all reverence, "By God, this is so." It was therefore a word never used lightly nor employed falsely.

"Amen" is the word Jesus used when he wished to stress a truth, the word translated in our Bibles as "Verily": "Amen, Amen, I say to you." It is the word used by pious Jews in Jesus' day when they responded to the synagogue prayers. It means "So let it be!" It is an act of final faith: God will bring it to pass. It is the glad surrender of the soul. I offer myself to God so that He may bring it to pass through me, if He so pleases.

"Amen" is a popular word in the religious vocabulary of people. In some churches the preacher might find his sermon punctuated by shouts of "Amen" from members of the congregation in response to something he has said. A preacher from the south who had this experience once related: "To say 'Amen' during a sermon is like saying 'sic em' to a dog chasing a cat. It encourages me in fighting the devil."

"Amen" also announces the termination of a prayer or sermon. But it terminates the prayer in a manner in which a signature terminates a check, or a mortgage, or a wedding license. One ought not to be reckless about the use of it, for it carries implications.

When we use the word "Amen" in terminating the Lord's Prayer, we add our voices to the voices of countless Christians who have testified to their faith in the Father to whom our prayer is addressed. In this final word, we add our own personal contribution and endorsement. It is our signature.

We should say it with force and power. By its use we claim the whole of the Lord's Prayer as our own. We affirm that what He has taught us to pray is really our own prayer. "Amen is a little word, but it takes a life—a dedicated life—to exhaust its meaning. In using it we are committing ourselves to the purpose for which we have prayed so that this purpose may become so in, through, and for us.

An old legend tells that when Jesus returned to heaven he was asked by an angel: "What have you left behind to carry out the work?" Jesus answered: "A little band of men and women who love me." "But what if they fail when the trial comes? Will all you have done be defeated?" "Yes," said Jesus, "if they fail all I have done will be defeated." "Is there nothing more?" "No," said Jesus, "There is nothing more." "What then?" Jesus quietly replied, "They will not fail."

The effect an "Amen" can have on a congregation was made known to me when I was preaching at an African-American congregation in Birmingham, Alabama. It so happened that I was participating with a number of other speakers, lay and clergy alike. I was the only white person on the platform. It was an exciting service, lasting over two hours. When my time came to speak I heard people shouting, "Amen," "Yes, brother," "Tell it like it is," and quite frankly, I became interactive with the congregation, and probably, spoke in a much more enthusiastic way than I otherwise would have done. Into the second hour there was one gentleman speaker who didn't seem to be "with it." The service dragged like a soufflé that hasn't been properly prepared—it sagged in the middle. He went on, droning away, when some dear woman in the back pew stood up and shouted: "Amen. Help him, Jesus. Help him, Jesus." And Jesus did help him and the service revived!

In the Old Testament, it was used as an exclamation. The Old Testament Jews were afraid of taking God's name in vain, so they would not use it. But, they very well might have said, "Amen." There is that phrase in Isaiah in which he talks about the God of amen. In the New Testament, there is a declaration that Christ is God's Amen to the world. Throughout the writings of Paul, "Amen" is often used to emphasize the certainty of something. In Jesus' teachings, he often used the word Amen, sometimes at the beginning of a phrase. I suspect that the King James translators did not know quite how to phrase Amen at the beginning of Jesus' teachings, so they translated it instead as "Verily I say to you". Verily, Verily I say to you. The text actually reads "Amen, Amen I say to you."

In fact, throughout the last 2000 years, Christians have used Amen as a means of devotion, as well as worship. After he was converted, Charles Wesley wrote in his journal, "I have been saved. Amen, Yes!" Charles went on to write that magnificent hymn, "Oh for a Thousand Tongues to Sing My Dear Redeemer's Praise." Actually, Charles Wesley wrote 19 total stanzas. We Presbyterians cannot handle that many, so in our book, we have it reduced to four. I have had a discussion with some musicians about this, and many Presbyterians have now omitted Amen entirely at the end of the hymn. Though, in our hymn book it is properly included, because Amen is more than the ending of a prayer or a hymn. It is a way of explaining to God, Yes, we thank you. In fact, if you look it up in your dictionary, you will read, "Amen means let it be. A way of affirming something that has been said. Let it be." I was reminded of this sometime ago when I was listening to a Beatles number by Paul McCartney: "Let It Be."

How do we say "Let it be" in worship? I think Amen should mean in worship that we want to participate. Too often in Christian worship I perceive we like to sit on the sidelines and watch someone else perform. We assume that there must be professional guidance in our Christian living. Now, while it is true that clergy have certain professional qualifications, yet in the church of Jesus Christ the apostle Paul says that it is like a body with many members and we all have gifts. Some teaching, preaching and ministering, calling: many gifts. Each one of you has a different gift. So, never let it be said that this church depends simply on professional leadership. We have elders and deacons and committee chairs and others who are likewise involved in leadership. I think professionalism has been over stated. You know the Titanic was built by professionals. The Ark was built by amateurs.

Sometimes we forget that one of the main doctrines of our Presbyterian faith is that of the Priesthood of all believers. That means that each one of us is to serve as a priest before God for ourselves and for one another. We all must find ways in which we may be able to participate. Sometimes the reason that I tell a story is to just get a response, and to get the attention of the worshippers. Laughter in the Presbyterian Church sometimes becomes an Amen on the part of the congregation. It lets the minister know others are listening. It lets me know the congregation is awake. It lets the minister know others are worshiping God as well. We all participate in Christian worship.

Someone who said this most clearly for me was a Danish philosopher 200 years ago, Soren Kierkegaard. He had a brilliant word about worship. He said of the worship in his day and the worship in our day, "When we come to worship, we assume that the ministers and the organist and the director and the choir are the leaders. The worshippers are those sitting in the pews listening." Not so at all. In God's mind, those at the front, the organist, the director, the clergy, the choir, are mere prompters behind the scenes. Center stage is the congregation. God is the audience, and by his Spirit, He is communicating with our spirits. He knows where worship is or is not occurring. Do we truly adore him? Do we confess our sins? Do we ask for our daily needs? Do we thank him for our many blessings? This is where the worship truly occurs.

Worship is a key word for me in participating together as Christians. I remember seeing a Saab automobile commercial. It has a fellow at the wheel; he is driving fast down the highway. As the picture fades out, there is a line over the top of the screen which reads, "Life is a participatory sport." In other words, you are to participate in the sport of life. Too often, we are like couch potatoes, sofa spuds, sitting waiting for some multimillion dollar athlete to perform for us so that we can applaud or hiss that person's performance. It reminds me of the English in India in the 19th Century Empire. The English did not want to get out in the hot sun, so they hired Indians to play tennis for them. We laugh at that. But who are we to hire ball players to play for us so that we can simply sit back and watch? Or hire clergy to worship for us?

I remember the 1954 Cotton Bowl game. It was being played between Notre Dame and Texas A&M. It was the fourth quarter. It was a hard fought game and the score was tied. A Notre Dame back was running up the sideline, heading for a touchdown when a third string guard from the Texas A&M bench suddenly ran out on the field and tackled him. The announcer asked, "Where did he come from?" He had ruined the play and he was suspended from further play. But, I would like to pin a medal on that fellow. He wanted to get into the action and participate in the game. He had not been able to before. Yes, life is a participatory sport.

But not only am I concerned that our worship should be one where we all participate together, worship also calls on us for affirmation. We affirm our faith with the Apostles' Creed, but affirmation involves much more than a repetition of a few words. Affirmation means that we assert what we truly believe in our own hearts. It is a positive statement. It is a likely statement of what is possible, what our potential is, what God's potential is within us and what he calls upon us to be. I cannot possibly imagine the effects of negativism and negative thinking on the Christian churches of America. Let one thing go wrong and there is always a chorus of people who raise negative voices.

I remember a story of Tony and Luigi. Luigi was a barber and Tony went to Luigi every month for his haircut. One month as Tony was sitting there, Luigi said, "Tony, what are your plans for this month?" And Tony said, "Well, I will tell you what, I am going to Rome."

"Rome?? How are you going to get there?"

"Well, I'm flying on TWA airlines."

"TWA? They are going bankrupt, and the seats are so crowded close together…"

"Well, I am going anyway."

"Where are you going to stay when you get there?"

"I am going to stay at the Helmsley Hotel."

"Helmsley? Leona Helmsley is ruining that hotel chain. They don't even give you chocolates on your pillow there anymore."

WHAT TO SAY WHEN WE PRAY:

"I don't care; I am going to stay there."

"What are you doing when you get to Rome?"

"We have an audience with the Pope."

"Audience, schmaudiance. There will be 200,000 people standing in St. Peter's Square, he won't see you or even know you are there."

"Well, we got the appointment anyway."

So, Tony went on his trip and a month later he came back for another haircut. Luigi says, "Well, how was the trip?"

"Wonderful!"

"How was TWA Airlines?"

"Wonderful, they had it overbooked so they pushed us up to first class. We got slippers for our feet and we got wine and we had steak to eat. It was marvelous."

"What about that Helmsley hotel?"

"Fantastic. They had also overbooked. There was a large soccer convention in town and so instead of getting a little room overlooking the alley, we got a suite at the top of the hotel, overlooking the river. It was marvelous."

"What about the Pope?"

"That is the best part of all. Because of the International Soccer Convention, people didn't show up for this big audience, so the few of us that were there were invited by the Papal guard to come up to his private chambers. There were not more than 10 or 15 of us standing there ready to greet the Pope. The Pope looked over at me and he said, "Tony, would you come up here for a minute please."

So I did. He said, "Tony, where in the world did you get that awful haircut?"

. . . . .

I can't tell you how easy it is to be negative. To be positive is something else. We affirm our faith, we get our batteries charged, we get a new look on life; we may make a decision for Jesus Christ, or to be a better Christian, or to live for him, or to help someone. In the context of worship, miracles can happen in our spirit, through the music, through the prayers, through the word, through the message. Things go on in our minds and in our hearts which can transform us.

When the Apostle Paul was speaking to the Corinthian Christians he said, "God, through all times and places, has made great promises. He has promised that he is love, he has promised forgiveness, and He has promised strength in sorrow; he has promised eternal life to us by faith." You and I may have doubted that, and been confused about that, may have felt kind of "yes" and kind of "no" and been uncertain. But, we need waver in uncertainty no longer because Jesus Christ is God's "yes." Jesus Christ is God's authentication of all that has been promised up until now. Whatever questions we have, whatever perplexities are ours, Jesus Christ is God's resounding "yes". The things I have told you are true. Yes is our "Amen" and this you may believe. So, as the congregation says "Amen" it is saying what our world needs terribly to hear, this I can bank my life on. My Amen is backed up by Jesus Christ, who went through it all: from the cross and the tomb to the resurrection.

The third thing is this: "Amen" is a sign of our fellowship, of our sharing the faith, or sharing our mutual burdens and woes, joys and dreams. Fellowship, as a word, is too readily bandied about and too lightly taken. It means, for many people, simply a few minutes after church when we shake a hand and drink a cup of coffee, and then be on our way. I

WHAT TO SAY WHEN WE PRAY:

don't minimize that, I thank God for every Christian friend we have in the fellowship of the church, and we thank God that, at times, it is like a fellowship that is from above, and we sing about the communion of saints and thank God for all this. The fellowship of the church can be a cure for our loneliness.

But, the Bible means not just sharing some ideas or conversation. It means having the deep things of life in common, it means caring who you are, and knowing where you are, and letting you know who I am, and letting you know what I believe, and sharing the joy of being Christians together. Fellowship is all that, and more. When we join together to say the "Amen" in unison, we are standing together saying: "This is what the Church stands for. We may be quite different from one another, we may see things differently, we may have different theological perspectives, different political perspective, different styles of life, but we are one in our deep prayers and hopes for one another." We hope we may strengthen one another and encourage one another and love one another in terms of our personalities meshing together in the spirit of the great "Amen."

In Nebraska, there is a tiny western town named Ogalala. On the outskirts of town there is a small railway station. Someone came in from the East one day, and said, "This isn't exactly Grand Central Station, is it?" The ticket agent said, "No, but we're on the same rail line as the Grand Central Station is." I don't care how small, or how remote you may feel in worshipping in any congregation. You and I are on the same line with Christians in Russia, and Korea, and Africa, and Malaysia, and Europe and America. I don't care how singular you may feel in worship, we are on the same line with Abraham and Sarah, Peter and Paul, Mary and your grandparents, and parents and mine, and Brewster, and Robinson, and Calvin, and Luther, and all the rest. We are on the same line. This is the assurance we have in the fellowship of kindred minds that is like that above.

There's one final word I'd like to share with you. When we say "Amen" it is not only a note of our participation, of our affirmation, and of our fellowship, but, also, of our dedication to what is being experienced and expressed. When we say "amen" we are saying we take our stand with whatever prayer is being spoken, and whatever hymn is being sung. We are saying that we give our assent to what this congregation believes and we are willing to take the consequences of this belief. That means, when the leader prays for peace, we agree to be peacemakers. When the leader asks God for healing, we must pray for the health of one another, and must visit one another, must hold one another up in our prayers for health and strength. God loves us and invites us into the family and into His presence. He accepts us as his children and that's what the Lord's Prayer is all about. He does not say, "Oh, you're going to have to be kept out in the waiting room, reading old Reader's Digest magazines while I make up my mind whether to admit you or not." Rather, he says: "Come in, my child, I love you, and I take you just as you are."

There was a conversation one morning as a mother awakened her son, and said: "Son, it's time for school." He responded: "But mother, I'm not going to go today, I'm going to call in sick." She said, "You can't do that." He replied: "Oh, the teachers don't like me, the kids don't like me, and even the people in the cafeteria don't like me." She said: "Son, you are going to go because they're expecting you, it is your job and because you're the principal of the school." Have you ever felt like calling in sick and pulling the covers up over your head, and saying, "I don't want to go today?" I want to stay home and feel sorry for myself. I don't want to get involved in the church, or the community, or my job or anything else.

Jesus Christ is the grand "A-men." "I'm willing to go on and get involved in this life." It's the "amen" that God has endorsed across the ages, and across the continents, written in the very tender language of one brief span of years, lived out for our sakes in love, and mirrored from that life, into our own. Jesus Christ becomes a better explanation of reality than anything else I can imagine in this world.

Years ago, they used to have in churches, an "amen corner." The preacher would plant several people there. They would be expected to shout "Amen!" at appropriate places. But, they finally got rid of it, and I'm glad they did, because everybody should be in the "amen corner," those who are in the back, those who are in the middle and those who are on the sides, because we are all to be involved in the "amen" of God's truth.

There is a current word which, maybe, comes closer to the ancient-sounding "Amen" and is used especially by young people. What they'll do if they agree with something, they'll say, "Yes!" And that's what I think the Apostle Paul is telling the people of Corinth. Jesus Christ is God's "Yes" to life itself. That's why the Psalmist ends with the words, "All God's people say 'amen.'" Say "Yes" to God.

As we conclude our thoughts on the Lord's Prayer, I hope we may say "Yes" to God when we utter this prayer all the rest of the days of our lives. Its use in liturgy is only a small part of it. Its use in life is far more significant. I hope we can say "Yes" to our commitment to the heavenly Father, who loves us in Christ, "Yes" to his holy name, which we honor and respect, "Yes" to his dream of the kingdom of God, "Yes to the doing of his will on earth. "Yes" to the sharing of the bread that he has given us to enjoy, "Yes" to God's idea of forgiveness, and "Yes" to our practice of that same kind of forgiveness, "Yes" to be led by him out of temptation, and "Yes" to be delivered from evil, "Yes" to him to whom is the kingdom, and the power and the glory forever!

As we do this the rest of our lives, we may hear God saying "Yes" to us as well. God does say "Yes" to us when we say "Yes" to him. God says "Yes, Yes" with a cosmic roar that opens that other door. At creation, God said, "Yes, let's splash the sky with light, let's float the Earth in space, let's dance away the night." And, God says "Yes, my child, yes." And God said, "Yes, let Jesus Christ be born, let's find him in the straw, let's blast the shepherd's horn." And God says, "Yes, my child, yes." And God said "Yes" to his broken son, and "Yes" to his many wounds, and "Yes" to the open tomb. God says "Yes, my child, yes." And God says, "Yes, we will leap the swirling sky, we will foil the hungry grave, we will never stop to die." And God says "Yes" to that other door. God says "Yes" when people say "No." "Yes, my child, love me evermore. And all God's people said together, "AMEN."

Prayer: *Help us, dear Father as we live our lives and say our prayers, to hear your divine "Amen" in ourselves. Amen.*

Brief Biography of
Dr. Robert E. Palmer

Dr. Robert E. Palmer, a native of Chicago, now resides with his wife Mary Lou in Celebration, Florida. After graduation from the University of Illinois and Princeton Theological Seminary, he received his Ph.D. Degree from the University of Edinburgh (Scotland), with additional studies at Cambridge and Oxford Universities.

He has served three large Presbyterian congregations in Santa Monica, California, Lincoln, Nebraska and Naples, Florida. He also served part-time at six churches prior to his ordination and 11 congregations as interim in his retirement.

Dr. Palmer also served as Associate Professor at the University of Nebraska and as Chaplain of the Nebraska Unicameral Legislature for 23 years.

As a distinguished Presbyterian Pastor Bob founded the Presbyterian Pastors' Large Church Conference more than a quarter of a century ago. It still continues to gather each year.

He has written several books, he had a Television Ministry and he has been the National Chaplain of the Alpha Tau Omega Fraternity.

The Doctors Palmer were married in 1950. They have four children and ten grandchildren.

DESERT MINISTRIES INC.
Current Publications Available

SOMETIME BEFORE THE DAWN: Responses to the Resurrection
- Dr. Richard M. Cromie

YOU NOW HAVE CUSTODY OF YOU:
Christian Reflections on Marriage and Divorce - Dr. Richard M. Cromie

WHEN YOU LOSE SOMEONE YOU LOVE
- Dr. Richard M. Cromie

WHEN A CHILD DIES - Dr. Daniel T. Hans

WHO REALLY LISTENS WHEN I SPEAK? - Jodie Huizenga

CHRIST WILL SEE YOU THROUGH - Dr. Richard M. Cromie

THE BEST IS YET TO BE - Dr. John Calvin Reid

PRAYERS AGAINST DEPRESSION - Dr. Lance Martin

RELECTIONS ON SUICIDE - Dr. Perry H. Biddle, Jr.

Recovery From Rape: **A JOURNEY INTO HOPE**
- Gretchen Howard

A Guidebook for a . . . **PASTOR SEARCH COMMITTEE**
- Dr. Glenn Doak

WHEN YOUR LIFE INCLUDES A WHEELCHAIR
- Marilyn Murray Willison

A TIME TO MOURN AND A TIME TO DANCE
- Evie McCandless

WHEN ALZHEIMER'S DISEASE STRIKES
- Dr. Stephen Sapp

A JOURNEY THROUGH CANCER
- Dr. Melanie Bone and Dr. Richard M. Cromie

DYING WITH GRACE AND HOPE - Dr. S. Allen Foster

RHAPSODY OF SCRIPTURE - Dr. Richard M. Cromie

MY COMMITMENT - Dr. John Calvin Reid

HOW TO HELP AN ALCOHOLIC - Martin

HUMOR AND HEALING - Dr. Perry H. Biddle, Jr.

Please visit our web site: www. Desmin.org